Getting Married in New Zealand – Te Mārenatanga ki Aotearoa

A guide to creating wedding and birth celebrations

Gregory Hughson
&
Douglas Pratt

Copyright © 2020 Gregory Hughson & Douglas Pratt

Except as noted below, this book or any portion thereof may not be reproduced or used in any manner whatsoever without the express written permission of the publisher except for the use of brief quotations in a book review.

Summaries, checklists and sample text of ceremonies may be copied and adapted, with acknowledgement of:
Getting Married in New Zealand – Te Mārenatanga ki Aotearoa: Gregory Hughson & Douglas Pratt (2020)

This book is a new, fully revised and updated edition of *Celebrating Marriage: A New Zealand guide to wedding ceremonies and birth celebrations*
by Douglas Pratt

International Print edition (2020)

ISBN 978-1-98-857265-9

Philip Garside Publishing Ltd
PO Box 17160
Wellington 6147
New Zealand

books@pgpl.co.nz

PDF, ePub and Kindle editions also available

Website for downloading free checklists and summaries:

www.pgpl.co.nz

Cover photograph:

Paul Hughson, taken at the outdoor Akaroa, New Zealand wedding of Johanna Hughson and Chris Stewart. (April 2012)

Contents

Preface 9
Acknowledgements 14
About the Authors 15
Part One – Getting Married 16
  1 — Introduction 17
  2 — Practical preliminaries 21
    Legal requirements 21
      Age limitation 21
      People previously married 21
      Place of marriage 21
      Time 22
      Witnesses 22
      Registry Office wedding option 22
      Marriage and Civil Union Blessings 23
      Marriage licence (Certificate of marriage) 23
      Marriage by proxy 24
      The banns / Formal announcement 24
      Objections to a marriage 24
    Four steps to getting married 25
      1. Decide who is to perform the ceremony 25
      2. Arrange for a place in which to get married 26
      3. Confirm that you are eligible to marry 26
      4. Obtain a marriage licence 26
    Expectations and duties 27
      1. The engagement 27
      2. The marriage relationship: preparation and counselling .. 28
      3. The type of wedding ceremony 29
      4. Invitations 29
      5. The bridal party 30

6. The role of the chief bridesmaid 31
7. The role of the best man 32
8. Gifts for your attendants 33
9. Decorations and apparel 33
10. The photographer 34
11. Social Media 35
12. Wedding gifts 35
13. Who pays – and for what? 35
14. The importance of a wedding ceremony rehearsal 36
15. Some other considerations 37

3 — The marriage ceremony: structure and plan 38

Multi-choice marriage ceremony 41
    Basic structure and item options 41
Section I – Setting the scene 42
    Item 1: Introduction 42
    Item 2: Prayer 49
    Item 3: Reading 52
Section II – The main action 60
    Item 4: Declaration of Intention 61
    Item 5: The Giving and Affirmation 64
    Item 6: The Vows 66
    Item 7. The Exchange of Rings 71
    Item 8: The Pronouncement 74
Section III – Drawing to a close 76
    Item 9: Readings on love 77
    Item 10: Conclusion 84
    Item 11: The Dismissal 87
    Item 12: The Blessing 88

Contents

4 — The reception: recipe for a wedding meal 91
- Simplicity 91
- Degrees of formality 93
- Reception Outline 94
  - 1. Commencement 94
  - 2. Toast to the marriage partners 94
  - 3. The marriage partner's speech 94
  - 4. Reply 95
  - 5. The best man's speech 95
  - 6. Other toasts 95
  - 7. Cutting of the cake 95
  - 8. Messages of congratulation 95
  - 9. The wedding meal 95
- Advice for all speakers 96

5 — Celebration and commitment: the honeymoon and beyond 97
- Seven keys to a healthy relationship 100
  - Communication 100
  - Acceptance 102
  - Sensitivity 103
  - Understanding 104
  - Respect 104
  - Mutual Support 105
  - Forgiveness 105
- Some relationship-building exercises 106
  - Share with each other 106
  - An exercise in touch 107
  - Learning to express feelings and reactions 107

Part Two – Marriage Records 109

- 1 — Planning your wedding: a practical guide 110
  - Preparation checklist 110
  - Marriage ceremony selection list 112
  - The reception: a summary..113
    - Style of wedding reception meal...............................113
    - Toasts and speeches 113
    - Cutting the cake 113
    - Reading of messages..113
    - Social time and/or dance option..............................114
  - Reception checklist 115
- 2 — Keeping Account:
  A wedding and anniversary record 116
  - Our Wedding Day..116
  - Our anniversaries...117

Part Three – Having Children..118

- 1 — Welcoming children 119
- 2 — Celebrating birth: ceremony formats........................... 123
  - Ceremony 1 123
    - Format options:..123
    - Introduction 124
    - A reflective reading or mediation 125
    - An act of promise by the parents..............................127
    - An act of promise by the Godparents 129
    - An affirmation by family and friends......................129
    - An act of blessing 130
    - Prayer of thanksgiving 130
    - The Lord's Prayer (*may be spoken together*)...........131
    - The Benediction 131
  - Ceremony 2 132
    - Format options:..132
  - Ceremony 3 134

Contents

Part Four – Same-Sex ceremonies **135**

  1 — A new development.. 136

  2 — Marriage ceremony resources and options 139

  3 — The blessing of same-sex marriage............................... 142

      Preliminary prayers 142

      The Blessing of the Couple 143

Part Five – Alternative language and religion options **146**

  1 — A Māori language ceremony
      Te ritenga karakia mō te Mārena 147

    Ngā Whakaritenga Mārena
    – order of marriage service/ceremony 148

    Te Whakaeke (the arrival process/ kawa of the Marae)......148

    Te Minita (Minister / Celebrant) 148

    He Mihi Whakatau (Welcome to the guests) 148

    Te Karakia (Prayers) 148

    Anei ētahi kōrero o ngā Karaipiture e pā ana ki te mārena (Scripture readings) 149

    Ngā Pātai (main questions to the couple) 151

    Kia inoi Tātou (prayer)..151

    Ngā Oati Tapu (Vows/oaths) 151

    Ngā Rīngi (The giving and receiving of rings) 152

    Te Whakapai (Prayer of Blessing)..........................153

    He Waiata (song or hymn) 153

    Te Inoi a Te Ariki (The Lord's Prayer) 153

    Te Waitohu i te Raihana Mārena (signing the marriage register) 154

    Te Whakatau (Declaration of Marriage)...............154

  2 — A Buddhist (Tibetan) marriage ceremony 155

    Wedding Format 155

3 — Muslim marriage ... 161
- The Nikah (Muslim marriage contract ceremony) ... 162
- Sample of a simple Muslim marriage contract: ... 162
- Vows and Blessings ... 163
- What Guests Should Wear to a Muslim Wedding ... 164
- The Bride's Wedding Outfit ... 164
- Separating Genders ... 164
- The Wedding Feast (Walima) ... 165

Appendices ... 166
- 1 — Hymn, song and musical options ... 166
- 2 — Website / Internet resources ... 169
- 3 — References ... 171
- 4 — Bibliography of same-sex resources ... 172

Preface

It is over three decades since *Celebrating Marriage: a practical guide to getting married in New Zealand* was first published by Benton Ross (Auckland, 1986). That book was subsequently revised and published as *Celebrating Marriage: a guide to New Zealand wedding ceremonies* by Random Century (Auckland, 1990) who had taken over the firm of Benton Ross. Both the first and second editions sold out. Ongoing requests for the book led to a third edition (ColCom Press, 1996) which was a light revision of the original. The last (6th) printing of the third edition was in 2012. Due to significant changes in New Zealand's marriage law to include same-sex marriage, and the availability now of a great deal of online marriage preparation material, the time has come for a fully revised, new version, in two formats – printed and electronic. The electronic as well as printed formats will enhance its more widespread availability and ease with which couples will be able to "cut and paste" their wedding ceremony from the options provided.

This new version comprises a significant update and revision led by Greg Hughson, building on the original text by Douglas Pratt. Both authors have had significant experience of helping couples prepare for marriage ceremonies and conducting ceremonies in Aotearoa-New Zealand over the last 40 years. Each has also been active in promoting interfaith activities and greater interreligious understanding in New Zealand and beyond. This book represents a pooling of their experience and expertise.

There is a great deal that we can learn from people who base their lives and marriages on a faith different to ours, or on no particular religious faith-foundation at all. Furthermore, in our experience, most people in Aotearoa-New Zealand have an appreciation of the importance of spirituality, if only due to the widespread acceptance of Māori spirituality within our contemporary cultural fabric. Many, if not most, couples in Aotearoa today would describe their marriage ceremony as a significant spiritual occasion.

We hope this new resource will be valued by all who seek a broader and more informed understanding of marriage. Accordingly, this updated resource provides some interfaith marriage ceremony options, as an aid to greater understanding.

Previous versions of this resource included a range of options for couples and celebrants to prepare ceremonies suited to each couple. The focus has always been on flexibility and appropriateness. This new edition enhances the flexibility further, providing ideas for the wording of same sex and te reo Māori ceremonies, and some examples of other-faith marriage ceremonies, alongside more traditional Christian and secular forms.

In this new edition, the words "Partners in Marriage" can be substituted wherever necessary for "Groom and Bride," where these traditional terms otherwise appear in the text. The move to legalise same-sex marriage in Aotearoa-New Zealand is historically significant. As a flow-on effect, the language of "being a couple" has changed – it no longer presumes a heterosexual pairing of male and female. And such couples increasingly refer to themselves as "partners" rather than "husband" and "wife." We have therefore provided some additional resources and reflections for those who may wish to study this development in more detail.

Also, given developments in Australia such as the recent endorsement of same-sex marriage by the Uniting Church, we hope that our book may be of value to couples seeking to be married in Australia, and elsewhere in the world. While designed primarily for a New Zealand setting, much of the ceremony content is easily transferable to other settings.

The format and style of the wedding reception has also evolved over the years. In this fully revised edition, we have made changes to the options and information previously provided. We have sought to take account of significant changes within society. The notion of "family" in Aotearoa-New Zealand, and indeed in Australia and elsewhere in modern Western secular societies, is far broader than it was 30-40 years ago. Committed relationships, of whatever form, are still acknowledged to be very important in our societies.

We provide this resource in the hope that it will assist couples and celebrants to create ceremonies that give expression to the unique relationship being celebrated and affirmed, in the best and most meaningful way for each couple.

Getting married is more than a legal transaction. It signifies and enacts a change to the relational and "spiritual" quality and significance of each couple's commitment. Marriage means a great deal more than the convenience of living together. Some people may choose not to marry in the legal sense but may wish to "celebrate" or otherwise publicly mark their own commitment to each other. Our aim is to help couples create a ceremony which will enable them to appropriately express their unique intentions and sincere commitment to each other. Indeed, what makes a marriage legal is not the substance of the celebratory ceremony, but the addition to it of the signing, with witnesses, of the marriage licence. In some countries these two components are kept apart – the legal dimension taking place at the appropriate civil office, often before but sometimes after, the wedding ceremony at a church or another setting.

Further, we acknowledge that not all valid partnerships are marriages. Choosing to live in a de-facto long-term partnership is no longer unusual. Not everyone wants or needs to mark their relationship commitment with a ceremony. But for those who do, hopefully the resources of this book will assist in creating a very special occasion.

We recognise that there are many different and varied contexts for marriages, and thus their celebration, in terms of the ever-increasing cultural and religious diversity in New Zealand, as elsewhere. For example, there is a contrast between a western-cultural style "nuclear family" and the Māori "whanau" or extended family. Of course, Pakeha (i.e. non-Māori) may also enjoy the context of wider family networks, and many Māori couples set up and value their "nuclear family." But cultural differences do exist, and not only those which distinguish Māori from Pakeha. There are also Fijian, Niuean, Samoan and Tongan, to name just four of the Pacific cultures now rooted deep into New Zealand soil. Indian, Cambodian, Chinese, Korean, Japanese, Vietnamese, and other variants of Asian and South East Asian cultures now add their unique dimensions to the multicoloured tapestry of New Zealand social life. In recent years this diversity has been enhanced by the arrival of significant numbers of South Africans – the Kiwi barbecue is just as likely today to be a 'braai' – and also former refugees from Africa, Syria, the Middle East and elsewhere.

It is both beyond the competency of the authors, and the scope of this resource, to specifically address all of the diverse cultural and religious contexts now present in Aotearoa-New Zealand. The diversity of types of wedding celebrations is now vastly greater than 30-40 years ago. Nevertheless, all couples who seek to marry under New Zealand law still need to take account of the legal requirements that are described in this book. Even if specific cultural or religious expectations dictate certain formalities and procedures to be followed, the legal requirements may mean some adaptation and modification of expectations are called for. In which case, this book may offer some helpful hints and advice. Our aim here is to be as inclusive as possible.

As with heterosexual unions, other committed relationships – Lesbian, Gay, Bisexual, Transsexual and Intersex (LGBTI) for example – are also widely celebrated today. In New Zealand, civil unions (for both heterosexual and homosexual couples) have been legal since 2005 and same-sex marriage since 2013. Furthermore, the diversity of family situations extends the idea of family far beyond notions of traditional marriage and the "nuclear family" – for example, the solo-parent family and the childless couple family, or families with non-heterosexual (LGBTI) parents. Since 2013, married same-sex couples have been able to adopt children jointly. Unmarried couples of any sex and couples in a civil union can now jointly adopt children, under a New Zealand High Court ruling in December 2015.

We have chosen, therefore, to include some wording options for same-sex marriage ceremonies and for the blessing of same-sex marriages. We also include some additional historical background on same-sex marriage (Part Four) We acknowledge that same-sex marriage will continue to be controversial, particularly within some religious communities. The information we provide is intended to foster ongoing respectful dialogue between people holding diverse opinions, as well as between people of different faiths.

The multi-choice marriage ceremony format in this book has been designed to assist couples to construct their own ceremony. All of the "standard" heterosexual options we have provided can be modified for same-sex ceremonies, or translated into Māori or other languages.

This new edition continues to include ceremonies of thanksgiving and blessing for the birth of a child. A marriage is primarily a relationship between two persons. It is not always certain or desirable that children will be born. Marriages with no children are nonetheless genuine marriages. However, many couples enter into a committed partnership with the intention of having, or adopting, a child, or children. The ceremony options we provide may be used whether or not the committed and loving parents of the child are heterosexual.

In preparing this book we have drawn from many sources. The numerous couples we have married have contributed by shaping the options for the marriage ceremony, just as you will shape yours. Enjoy your day, your ceremony, your marriage! It is yours to make of it as you will.

Gregory Hughson and Douglas Pratt
October 2020

Acknowledgements

We would like to sincerely acknowledge the contributions made to this new edition by Rev Dr Wayne Te Kaawa (Māori marriage ceremony), The Uniting Church of Australia (Same-sex marriage ceremony, 2018), Imam Gamal Fouda, Imam of the Al Nur Mosque in Christchurch, Hilda Hughson (for help with Māori language and general proof reading), Dr Najib Lafraie (Muslim marriage information) and Dr Joe Llewelyn and Lama Yeshe (Buddhist ceremony). Thank you also to Rev Howard Leigh for providing access to *The Way Forward* 2016 same-sex marriage Anglican Church blessing material, and to Rochelle Fleming, New Zealand Marriage Celebrant, for information relating to the welcoming of children.

Comments and information about legal aspects in the New Zealand context are based on the appropriate Marriage Act and supporting material provided by the New Zealand Department of Justice and the Department of Internal affairs.

About the Authors

Gregory Hughson

With an M.Sc. in Biological Science and from a background in Agricultural Science Research, Greg trained for ordination as a Methodist Minister from 1985-1987, obtaining a Bachelor of Divinity in Practical Theology with Distinction from the University of Otago. He spent six years in parish ministry in Feilding (1988-93) followed by six years as Methodist Parish Superintendent in Gisborne (1994-99). He spent the next twenty years (2000-2019) as ecumenical chaplain at the University of Otago. Throughout his ministry Greg has enjoyed conducting many weddings, largely based on material provided by Douglas Pratt in previous editions of this book. Greg is now retired and living in Dunedin.

Douglas Pratt

Douglas trained as a Methodist minister, gaining degrees in philosophy (MA) and theology (BD, PhD). He later trained as a marriage relationship counsellor and supervisor. It was during his first parish appointment, 1975-78, that Doug began to offer a multi-choice marriage ceremony format and was at the forefront of promoting alternatives for both the ceremony and the location of weddings. Such developments paved the way for today's context of secular (Civil) marriage celebrants. In 1984, following two years of overseas study (1979-80) and three years in Methodist parish ministry in Dunedin (1981-83), Doug took up an appointment as ecumenical chaplain to the University of Waikato. In 1988 he was appointed the foundation lecturer in Religious Studies at the University. In 1998 Doug became an Anglican priest while remaining a full-time university lecturer, retiring in 2018 as a professor. It was during his tenure as chaplain that the initial work on alternative marriage ceremonies was further developed and led to publication.

Part One – Getting Married

1 — Introduction

People choose to get married for some or all of the following reasons; love, companionship, sexual fulfilment, togetherness, mutual support, security, or to fulfil family or societal expectations. People choose to get married in many different circumstances and stages of life. Young adults on the threshold of life, full of exuberance and expectation; couples where one or both are re-marrying, where the hurt and sadness resulting from a lost relationship through death or dissolution are being laid to rest in the hope of life in new partnership; older folk who, in their autumnal years, have found a special companion preferable to solitude. Whatever the circumstance, whatever the stage in life, the decision to marry is a major one. Marriage is an act of profound relational, "spiritual" and personal commitment. Having made the decision, the next task is to organise an event whereby the decision to get married can be celebrated.

The process of preparing for marriage and for getting married can be quite demanding. Among the many practical tasks that have to be undertaken, working together with your celebrant to prepare an appropriate ceremony will be very important.

For your ceremony to be meaningful and significant, the words you choose need to express what you truly feel, believe and hope for. This book is designed to help you make the best choice of wording for your marriage ceremony, as well as offering some practical advice and guidelines on many other matters associated with your ceremony and wedding day. We also address some wider relationship matters beyond the wedding itself, including keys to a healthy relationship and some ceremonies celebrating the birth of a child and/or the blessing of children.

This book does not pretend to be the last word on weddings, nor on ways of celebrating the birth of a child. We seek rather to provide a practical resource for couples, with a particular focus on wording options for the marriage ceremony itself. It is our hope that out of the options offered you will find words which "ring true" for you; that you can use or modify as appropriate for your unique ceremony. Creating a marriage ceremony is like creating a work of art. It takes a great deal of time and careful preparation. But it is worth it. Together, as a couple, you have the opportunity to create not only a suitable ceremony, but an experience which you will remember and treasure for many years to come.

Church ministers are available as marriage celebrants. Alternatively, you can find a Civil marriage celebrant online here:

https://www.celebrantsassociation.co.nz/

There will be many marriage celebrants, both religious and non-religious, who will have other thoughts and suggestions based on their experience. And there are many celebrants who will be happy to offer you the choice of a self-constructed ceremony such as is offered here. This book provides some options and will, we trust, offer couples and their celebrant a starting point.

Whether or not you desire a religious ceremony, you will want to incorporate personally significant wording, movement and music into your service. We encourage you, with support from your celebrant, to work together to create a truly meaningful, memorable and joyful ceremony. Together you can create a beautiful event that expresses your sense of the mystery and wonder of life and love, a ceremony which gives expression, shape and texture to your own understandings of marriage and commitment. To prepare together for your marriage ceremony provides you with an opportunity to grow in your understanding of – and love for – each other. Some couples spend up to a year, sometimes even longer, preparing their ceremony. Some have less time. It is the quality of preparation that matters.

The structure and the format of wedding ceremonies that may be created from the templates provided in this book generally reflect and derive from a broadly Christian tradition and also secular post-Christian contexts. We have chosen also to include some "other-faith" (Muslim and Buddhist) material, to provide some insight into the religious diversity that is far greater in NZ today than 40 years ago. We cannot presume to offer a full suite of diverse religious and cultural formats. Rather, the multi-choice format of the ceremonies offered should cater for most circumstances. From the overtly religious to the distinctly secular, the point is not to what extent a ceremony conforms with a particular religious viewpoint, but to what degree it authentically celebrates the relationship of the couple who are marrying.

In the course of preparing many couples for their wedding, two things have stood out for us. The first is the need for a ceremony that is meaningful and appropriate. This book incorporates the result of many years' experience of offering couples a multi-choice format upon which to construct their marriage ceremony. The essence is flexibility and adaptability to individual circumstances. It forms the core of this book.

The second is the need for a reception that is enjoyable, a gathering and that "works" in terms of speeches, toasts, etc. Over the years, we have found ourselves offering the same basic advice concerning the format of wedding receptions. And having attended the receptions of many of the weddings we have taken, we have built up a clear impression of what makes for a good one, and what kinds of things can cause embarrassment! We explore this topic more fully in Section 4 of Part One.

Although the ceremony and reception are the focal points, we have also included information on legal aspects and practical matters that you need to attend to prior to actually getting married. A wedding always marks a new beginning in a relationship. Whatever the personal history and circumstances of the people involved, getting married always implies some measure of adjustment. Even if nothing appears to have changed in terms of day-to-day living, the context of that living has been altered. A marriage is first and foremost a relationship between two people who love each other. Living together, being friends, being lovers, are also relationships. Marriage embraces all of these, yet is more besides. Essentially this "more" is to do with a publicly declared commitment. This commitment requires a desire and a willingness to work at the deepening the relationship over many years. Section 5 of Part One therefore discusses some aspects relevant to the development, deepening and strengthening of your marriage relationship.

Part Two includes a planning checklist covering all the items you need to attend to before the wedding, and a form where you can record the options you have selected to construct your own ceremony. We have also included a brief summary of points that might be helpful in planning your reception, or "wedding breakfast." There is also a place where you can keep an appropriate record of your wedding, and of your anniversaries. Many couples choose to arrange a ceremony of "reaffirmation of marriage vows" on significant anniversaries of their marriage. Your minister, priest or civil celebrant can assist you with preparing for such a ceremony, should you so wish.

Part Three, "Having Children," offers some resources for rituals to celebrate the birth of a child.

Part Four contains specific resources for same-sex marriage ceremonies, and the blessing of same-sex marriages that have already taken place.

Part Five provides a few alternative language and religion options.

2 — Practical preliminaries

When it comes to preparing for the wedding day, there are many "do's" and "don'ts" that you will hear from family and friends. Some advice you receive will be helpful. Some will not be helpful. Use your common sense. Be appropriately assertive with others, to ensure that your ceremony, your day, "rings true" for you.

There is no golden rule that lays down exactly how everything should be done. There are certain traditions and guidelines to draw upon. These can be modified in accordance with changing circumstances and the realities of everyday life. If custom and tradition work for you, and are appropriate, fine. If not, then do what you think is best for you. This is the philosophy that undergirds our multi-choice approach to marriage ceremonies and reception guidelines

There are a few practical things that you need to be aware of concerning getting married in New Zealand.

Legal requirements

Age limitation
The minimum legal age for marriage is sixteen years, and people under twenty years of age at the time of marriage require the formal consent of their parent(s) or guardian(s).

People previously married
People who have been previously married are required to produce evidence that the former marriage has been legally dissolved before a licence for the new marriage can be issued.

Place of marriage
A wedding ceremony can take place anywhere, but, wherever it is to be, the location is stated on the licence and that is where it must be held. However, an alternate location can be given also on the licence.

This is of particular value if you wish to have an outdoor ceremony but, if the weather is bad, it will require you to go to another location. However, if you decide to change both the main location as well as the alternative location after you obtain your licence, then you must inform the Registrar of Marriages who issued your licence, before the ceremony takes place.

Time

Weddings may take place at any time between 6 am and 10 pm. Weddings may take place on any day, unless you wish to have a Registry Office wedding, in which case there are more restrictions on day and time.

Witnesses

A marriage ceremony must be performed in the presence of at least two witnesses. Only two are required to sign the legal documents at the wedding— usually they are the best man and the chief bridesmaid. There is no age restriction on the witnesses who sign. They just need to be mature enough to understand what they are doing.

Registry Office wedding option

This consists of a basic legal ceremony, which takes place in the presence of a Registrar and two or more witnesses. It takes place in the office of the Registrar, and normally during office hours. Each partner declares to the Registrar that there is no known legal impediment to their marrying. They then they declare to each other that they take each other to be their lawful wife, husband or partner. There is a fee for the Registrar's services and for a copy of the marriage certificate.

A new version of the registry ceremony vows has recently been approved. The Celebrants Association of New Zealand has provided a more contemporary version, taking away some of the more difficult language for those whom English is not their first language. This is available online via:

> https://www.govt.nz/organisations/births-deaths-and-marriages/.

Marriage and Civil Union Blessings

A marriage or Civil Union that has been performed in a Registry Office may be "solemnised," blessed, or otherwise celebrated, in a church or elsewhere at any later time. Same-sex marriages that have been conducted in a Registry office may now be blessed by clergy of some denominations, including some New Zealand Anglican and Methodist churches, in a ceremony held in a church or elsewhere. Instead of handing a marriage licence to the minister or celebrant, the couple must present the Registrar's certificate of marriage. Thus, the ceremony is not recorded (in the church wedding register or elsewhere) as another marriage.

Marriage licence (Certificate of marriage)

A licence issued by the Registrar of Births, Deaths and Marriages must be obtained before your wedding. You can apply for a marriage licence online via:

> https://www.govt.nz/browse/family-and-whanau/getting-married/get-a-marriage-licence/

A marriage licence currently (in 2020) costs $150, if you use a celebrant. A registry ceremony costs $240 in total. You need to arrange your licence at least 3 working days before you get married, and it expires after 3 months. Only one of you needs to complete the application, but you need information about both of you.

A marriage licence is the permit that enables a celebrant to perform a particular marriage ceremony as a legal wedding. You will receive two copies. During the ceremony, both copies of the licence are signed by the couple, by two witnesses and by the Celebrant. The bride signs her "maiden" (own) name as recorded on the licence. The subsequent (optional) use by the bride of the husband's surname is a matter of tradition, not a legal requirement or consequence of being married. You may also sign a church marriage register, or a register in the possession of your Civil celebrant. You will receive one copy of the licence from your celebrant after the ceremony. This is the document, signed by yourselves and your two witnesses, that you must keep to prove the legality of your marriage. A marriage performed without a licence, or by an unauthorised celebrant, is void.

The celebrant is responsible for scanning and emailing the other copy to the Registrar. The celebrant receives an email to confirm it has been received. Additional certified copies of Marriage Certificates can be ordered and obtained from the Registrar General's Office in Wellington.

Marriage by proxy

A marriage by proxy (where someone else stands in for the person getting married) may occur only when one of the partners intending to marry is unable to be in the country because of a state of war or armed conflict, or other compelling reasons. The person absent must provide written consent and appoint his/her proxy who stands in for the legal formalities. The writing of the consent must also be witnessed overseas by a legal representative.

The banns / Formal announcement

Publication of the banns announcing the forthcoming marriage is not a legal requirement. It is ancient custom that very few people choose to follow these days. This practice consists of a special announcement being made at the couple's church for three consecutive Sunday's prior to the wedding. Traditionally, this served to publicise the wedding and to provide an opportunity to support or challenge the couple's decision to marry. A modern version of this traditional formality is a public announcement on social media.

Objections to a marriage

Any person who wishes to object to a proposed marriage may lodge a written objection, called a caveat, with the Registrar of Marriages. This will mean the licence applied for cannot be issued until either the caveat is withdrawn or the objection is referred to the District Court for adjudication. Some traditional Church marriage ceremonies provide an opportunity for anyone present at the service to object to the marriage, during the service. We are unaware of any time when a marriage service has been obstructed by someone sincerely taking advantage of this opportunity to block the proceedings. Such an opportunity to object is rarely included these days. We would advise against this practice as it would introduce unnecessary anxiety for everyone present. Some unwise attendees may take the opportunity to attempt to interject with a "humorous or insincere objection." Far better to give everyone present the opportunity to fully affirm the couple in the decision they have made to marry.

Four steps to getting married

Now that you are acquainted with the basic legal facts and guidelines, let's look at the four practical steps you need to take in order to get married.

1. Decide who is to perform the ceremony

Do you want a Registry Office ceremony and hence a Registrar? Or a church ceremony with a minister (priest/pastor or chaplain)? Or a secular civil celebrant? Or a minister who is prepared to perform meaningful religious ceremonies in places other than a church? Or a person from another faith who is a registered marriage celebrant? You can find a religious or independent civil celebrant at:

   https://celebrants.dia.govt.nz/

Or you can contact your local Registry office, for a Registry Office ceremony.

Christian clergy celebrants (ministers of religion) are found by contacting the church or religious community of your choice, or via the website above. Type the denomination of the minister into the search box provided. All currently licensed independent marriage celebrants are also listed online, accessible via the link above.

The name of your chosen celebrant is entered on the licence thereby giving authority to the celebrant to perform your wedding. However, it does not legally oblige the celebrant to conduct the ceremony. The licence is transferable to another registered celebrant, should your celebrant for whatever reason, be unavailable on the day.

2. Arrange for a place in which to get married

Traditionally, the location at which the wedding takes place is the bride's choice, and because traditionally her parents are the hosts for the wedding, and in particular the reception, weddings very often take place in the bride's home town or suburb. However, whether it is the bride alone or both partners who decide, a suitable venue must be arranged. There are many Christian clergy, as well as other religious leaders and independent celebrants who are willing to marry people in all sorts of different locations. For example, in a park, in a garden, in a private residence, in a church, mosque, synagogue, temple, Buddhist centre; or on a boat, on a mountain, in a restaurant, and so on. Depending on your priorities, it is your responsibility to decide where you want to be married and then find a celebrant who is willing to marry you there.

3. Confirm that you are eligible to marry

You will need to confirm that you are not married already, that you are both in fact old enough (at least sixteen years of age) and that you are not in certain close kinship relationships with each other. For example, a man can't marry his aunt, nor a woman her uncle. See the full list here:

https://marriages.services.govt.nz/

4. Obtain a marriage licence

A Registry Office wedding does not require the prior issue of a licence before the wedding takes place. However, a wedding to be performed by a marriage celebrant requires you to obtain a licence from the Registrar of Marriages prior to your ceremony. See

https://www.govt.nz/browse/family-and-whanau/getting-married/get-a-marriage-licence/.

A licence is issued in the name of your chosen marriage celebrant. Without it, your celebrant cannot legally marry you. You need to ensure your marriage celebrant receives the licence in good time, at least a day or two before the wedding, if not sooner. Don't forget to allow at least three working days (preferably a few weeks) between your application for the licence and when you want it by.

In Muslim marriages, the bride and groom sign a sacred marriage contract in addition to their New Zealand legal marriage licence. This is something that all couples (religious or not) may like to consider, as it can provide a more meaningful and detailed record of all your intentions, than the legal licence. Preparing such a non-legal relationship, or spiritual, contract together provides each of you with a written record of mutual promises concerning the life you intend to share together as a married couple. You can create your own unique contract, with support from your celebrant.

Expectations and duties

Now let's look at the other main tasks every couple needs to attend to before the wedding can take place. The following outline of expectations and duties is a basic guideline only. Your personal circumstances will dictate certain changes or modifications, but this outline should be useful as you prepare for your wedding and help you allocate responsibilities. The key is to plan well ahead together, with your celebrant, so as to achieve a relatively smooth, trouble-free wedding day.

1. The engagement

Preparations for a wedding begin with the decision to marry. Many couples will choose to make a public announcement of their intention to marry, via social media and/or in a local newspaper. Many will choose to purchase an engagement ring or rings, to wear as a sign of mutual commitment and preparation.

There is no set time that an engagement should last. You need to allow enough time to plan and prepare for your wedding without any undue rush. The length of the engagement really depends on when it is appropriate and convenient for you to get married. Naturally, it is customary and courteous to inform your immediate families first. Often, couples will send out a "save the date" notice, before sending a formal invitation later. We recommend formal invites are sent out at least three months before the ceremony to give family and friends plenty of time to make travel arrangements.

Unless you want to marry on the quiet, weddings are very much family affairs. The support, encouragement and practical help of both families (ideally) can contribute significantly to the overall success, happiness and satisfaction of your wedding day. Whether you are living with each other, with your parents still, or in accommodation separate from each other, the engagement period is a time for both thinking and planning towards the marriage ceremony, and preparing for the new relationship that getting married implies. It is also a time to make sure that you have made the right decision to marry; an opportunity to reflect and confirm your intentions – or decide it is best not to proceed.

2. The marriage relationship: preparation and counselling

Some celebrants and faith community leaders offer, or can help you enrol for, a pre-marriage course for couples. The content will vary according to the perspective of whoever is offering the course. Such courses usually focus on developing and deepening the practical, emotional and spiritual skills needed to relate well to each other. There are many faith-based and secular couple's counselling courses available for those who are preparing to marry or have recently married.

Generally, such courses or consultations are very down-to-earth and practical in their approach. The aim is to help your relationship and marriage commitment to deepen and flourish in the long-term, and to help you be more certain that you are making the right decision.

Working with your partner and/or in small groups, you will have the opportunity to explore your expectations, attitudes and feelings, along with discussions including sexual intimacy, communication, listening skills, marriage roles, time management, stress management and financial budgeting. Preparation for marriage also often provides you with the opportunity to reflect on your parents' marriages. It is important to decide how much of your parents' example you are going to intentionally copy, or reject, in your own marriage.

We recommend that all couples who are preparing to marry, or couples who are recently married or living together, make use of such courses and consultations, particularly courses on listening skills and communication. See some helpful resources here:

https://prepare-enrich.co.nz/articles/articles-for-couples

Should significant problems occur after you are married, there are many relationship counselling services available to help you deal with issues and chart the right way forward. For counselling and support options in your area, see:

https://www.govt.nz/browse/family-and-whanau/separating-or-getting-divorced/relationship-counselling/

3. The type of wedding ceremony

A decision to be made early on is what type of wedding you want. What is your style? What is going to feel right for you? A highly formal affair? A semi-formal occasion? Something quite informal? Is a Cathedral the right setting? A church? A garden? A mosque? Synagogue? Some other form of religious centre? Some non-religious location – a sports club, for example? Or a favourite outdoor spot? The decision about the type of wedding ceremony you want will influence many other decisions such as the location, ceremony format, reception style, and so on.

4. Invitations

Once you have confirmed the place, date and time of your wedding, you will need to draw up a guest list. This is usually done in consultation with your parents or with whoever is hosting your wedding day. At the same time, you need to attend to preparing and sending invitations. There are many different styles and layouts to choose from. A stationer or printer will advise you on the options currently available. Alternatively, there are many online templates which you can download and send electronically or via post.

If you, as a couple, are hosting the wedding and reception yourselves, then the invitation is issued in your name. If the bride's parents are the hosts, then they issue the invitation. If, for whatever reason, it is another relative or person who is hosting the wedding, then the invitation should be issued in their name. Be sure that you provide a means of reply so that the person who receives the invitation can let you know whether or not they are able to attend.

5. The bridal party

Early on in your planning process you will need to choose your attendants. At the very least you need two people who will come forward as legal witnesses, even if you choose to dispense with the traditional bridal party. Sometimes the best man and chief bridesmaid or matron of honour (a chief bridesmaid who is herself married) act as the two legal witnesses. But any close friends or family members can be your two legal witnesses to sign the marriage register.

The size of the bridal party is purely a matter of choice, but don't forget the practicalities relating to the place where you are to be married and also the costs involved in having a larger group. You might not be able to fit a party of bride and groom, best man and three groomsmen, four bridesmaids, a page boy and two flower-girls across the front of the church or whatever indoor venue you are planning to use.

However many you choose to have, the two key attendants are the best man and chief bridesmaid or matron of honour. Groomsmen and extra bridesmaids are largely for show, although they can share in the duties that the best man and chief bridesmaid would otherwise have to perform alone. Normally, the best man is a close friend or relative of the groom, as are any groomsmen he chooses to have. Similarly, bridesmaids are generally sisters of the bride and groom, or close friends of the bride, with the chief bridesmaid having a clear place of honour and responsibility.

Flower-girls and page-boys, should you choose to have both or either, are usually selected from young nieces or nephews, or friends, on either side.

The traditional "line abreast" positioning of the bridal party is as follows:

- The bride stands to the left of the groom. The chief bridesmaid stands to the left of the bride. To her left stand any other bridesmaids, ending with the flower-girl(s).

- The best man stands to the right of the groom, and to his right stand the other groomsmen, ending with the page-boy(s).

If you are to be married in a less formal setting than a traditional church, you may wish to think about other ways of positioning the bridal party for the ceremony. For example, instead of the guests looking at the back of the bridal party, and hardly getting to see what is going on, let alone making out what bride and groom say to each other, why not try facing the invited guests in the form of a semi-circle. The bride and groom would be positioned in the centre, the celebrant to the left and forward of the groom, and the attendants in a group positioned to the right of the bride in such a way that the chief bridesmaid remains, nonetheless, the closest to the bride. The celebrant is in a position to speak out towards the guests and also, where appropriate, turn to address directly the bride and groom. It makes for a more intimate wedding, with a greater sense of sharing by all who attend. Variations on this configuration can be used in most churches as well as other settings.

6. The role of the chief bridesmaid

The chief bridesmaid is the bride's companion. If the bride is a little nervous and anxious, the chief bridesmaid should be calm and reassuring. She assists in dressing and preparing the bride, and ensures she is as relaxed as possible. It is her responsibility to ensure that the bride makes a dignified entry to the church, or wherever the wedding is taking place.

Traditionally, the bride is "escorted down the aisle" on the arm of her father. This has been critiqued in recent years as an example of a patriarchal practice from days long gone, an archaic practice which now should be avoided. We believe, however, that this critique need not prevent a father from engaging in this way, alongside his dearly loved daughter. If a father is not available, or unable for whatever reason, another special relative or friend can escort the bride during the bridal procession

Usually, the bridal party will precede the bride, helping build a sense of anticipation in those attending the ceremony. In this case, make sure that you leave a good interval between those who process in, so that the bridal party does not obscure the bride's entry.

During the ceremony the chief bridesmaid must be alert to take the bride's bouquet (if she has one) at the appropriate moment and also, where applicable, to take the bride's gloves and assist with the lifting of the veil, if there is one. She can also be one of the two witnesses to sign the register, and at the close of the ceremony she follows the newly-weds, on the arm of the best man, as they leave the church or other venue. At all times it is her responsibility to ensure the comfort and best appearance of the bride, both at the ceremony and also at the reception.

7. The role of the best man

The best man is charged with the responsibility of acting as companion and helper to the bridegroom. Together with any other groomsmen, he will accompany the bridegroom to the place of the wedding, ensuring that all arrive in good time, and in good condition. A wedding is a legal ceremony and cannot proceed if the parties to it are under the influence of alcohol, or other drugs. Both partners need to be fully alert and aware of the significance of the vows they will make, and be able to remember the ceremony afterwards.

Normally, the best man has the ring, or rings, in his possession ready to hand to the celebrant at the appropriate point in the ceremony. He may also be one of the two legal witnesses who sign the register. At the conclusion of the ceremony he escorts the chief bridesmaid as they exit following the newlyweds. The best man often takes on responsibilities to do with arranging transport. Certainly, he is expected to play an active role in many of the practical organisational tasks on behalf of the bride and groom. Unless the couple have attended to it in advance, it is normally the best man's task to see that fees or donations are paid to the celebrant, the organist, the church, and so on. We recommend that you discuss these costs or donations with your celebrant early on in your preparations.

At the reception the best man is usually the one to read the messages of congratulation, a task often shared with a groomsman. He may be called upon to speak, and possibly to respond to the toast to the bridesmaids. Finally, the best man should be the one to ensure the successful departure of the couple on their honeymoon.

8. Gifts for your attendants

It is customary to give both the best man and the chief bridesmaid a special gift in appreciation of their support and assistance. Also, you may like to consider a suitable gift for any other attendants you may have as part of your bridal party.

9. Decorations and apparel

Under instructions from the bride and her family, close friends and family members usually decorate the church or wedding ceremony venue. Some churches have an experienced group of people who will do this for you in return for a suitable donation. If you tell them the colour scheme you want, they will do their best to arrange flowers to suit. The floral decor of the place of marriage is generally arranged to complement the bouquets carried by bride and bridesmaids. The mothers of the bride and groom may also wear complementary corsages. A wedding would be a dull affair without the sparkle and colour of flowers. Whether you have this aspect of your wedding day taken care of professionally or by competent friends or family, some thought needs to be given to colour and style.

Together with flowers and decor, clothing completes the "look" of a wedding. White is the traditional bridal colour. Bridal boutiques and magazines will give up-to-the-moment detail of styles and fashions. Bridesmaids' frocks are usually designed in a style that complements the wedding dress and in a colour that harmonises with, or perhaps determines, the overall colour scheme of flowers, etc. Similarly, the groom and his attendants generally wear suits, either their own or hired ones, that tone in with the colour scheme that has been chosen. It's all a matter of personal taste, but the guiding principle is to achieve harmony and balance as far as visual appearances are concerned. Do bear in mind that choosing clothes and wedding rings, as well as whatever else you may wish to have to set the scene for your wedding takes time. Don't leave it all to the last minute!

10. The photographer

Many couples choose to employ a professional wedding photographer. When so much care and effort has gone into arranging your special occasion, you will also want to ensure a photographic record is created to enjoy for many years to come. A good photographer achieves this, with discretion. A wedding ceremony is not performed for the photographer's benefit, and although most celebrants will be happy to accommodate photos at certain points during the ceremony, especially during the signing of the marriage register, no one likes a photographer who dominates and interferes with the flow and dignity of the ceremony. So, choose your photographer carefully and make your instructions clear. It is advisable that your photographer attends your wedding practice, which is often held the day before the wedding ceremony.

Photos are usually taken at the place from which the bride departs, before the wedding; at the point of arrival at the church or place of wedding; at points during the ceremony (with the agreement of celebrant, bride and groom); immediately following the ceremony; and very often also at a more formal session, either indoors or outdoors, between the ceremony and reception. The photographic record is complete with the cutting of the cake. Sometimes this is "arranged" in a mock ceremony just prior to the reception so that the photographer does not have to wait around, often at considerable expense, until that moment in the proceedings arrives.

You may wish to employ your photographer to take a sequence of candid shots at the reception, so you can include a record of your guests in your wedding album. The advent of digital photography now means that couples can be assured of the quality of their photos, on the day of their wedding.

It is now common practice for digital video recording of the wedding ceremony to be arranged, as well as still-photography. Photos and videos taken of wedding ceremonies become increasingly precious over the years following the ceremony. They provide a priceless insight for generations to come, into the historic marriages of parents, grandparents and family members.

11. Social Media

Celebrants will normally announce at the beginning of the ceremony that no wedding or reception photos taken by guests be put on Facebook or other social media, until after the couple have posted their own specially chosen photos. So, consider whether you would like to ask your celebrant to make such an announcement.

12. Wedding gifts

People invited to a wedding normally send or bring a gift, whether or not they can attend in person. Most people like to think they are giving the couple something they need. It's not much fun if you discover you have just given the sixth toaster! In order to help people who inquire, it is helpful to draw up a "wish list." Write down the things you need and/or would like to receive and make this available to your invited guests. People can then let you know that they will give a particular item yet still retain the freedom of choice as to quality, brand and style of that item. Some companies have an online wedding gift register from which your guests can choose gifts. You can provide a link to such a site, with your wedding invitation.

Recording the gifts received, and issuing a personal acknowledgment is important. You may like to ask a friend or family member to compile such a list for you. We suggest that you send out notes of thanks for gifts received a few weeks after your wedding day.

On the wedding day, it is customary to display the gifts received, at the reception venue. Sometimes the guests are invited to the bride's home (or other venue) to view the gifts during a morning tea or barbeque lunch with the couple the day after the wedding. For security reasons, it is a good idea to have someone reliable remain with the gifts while everyone is at the wedding.

13. Who pays – and for what?

Weddings cost money. They can cost a lot of money, especially if you choose to use professionals such as a photographer, catering, cars, drivers etc. Weddings will cost less money if you are able to draw on the love and resources of friends and family. Traditionally, the bride's parents pay for the reception. These days however, both families, and the couple themselves, often share the cost.

The bridegroom is primarily responsible for attending to all fees (e.g. to the church, organist/pianist or other musician, marriage celebrant); bouquets for the bride and her attendants; corsages and buttonholes for the respective parents and the groom's attendants; the engagement ring and the wedding ring(s); and the gifts for all attendants.

The cost of the bridesmaid's attire, whether bought, made or hired, is usually the responsibility of the bridesmaids themselves. However, the bride and her family may contribute to all or part of this expense. Similarly, if the men are to dress in hired outfits, then it may be appropriate for the bridegroom to offer to pay all or part of the hire cost.

14. The importance of a wedding ceremony rehearsal

The importance of a rehearsal for your ceremony cannot be emphasised enough. A rehearsal is essential to enable you to feel as confident as possible on your wedding day that all will go well. The rehearsal provides an opportunity to gather and to run through the entire ceremony, under the guidance of your celebrant. The timing will depend on when the entire wedding party is able to gather. The rehearsal is generally held the day before the ceremony at the place where the ceremony will be held, so that learnings and clarifications are still fresh in everyone's minds the following day.

The rehearsal provides an opportunity for the release of a significant amount of stress and nervous emotion. The best rehearsals contain laughter. Inevitably, you will be feeling somewhat stressed, having prepared for such a significant occasion for so long. The rehearsal generally will help you prepare well, so that you can approach your wedding ceremony feeling relaxed, organised and open. Not everything can be rehearsed, but it is important that you have a clear understanding of what is going to happen on the day. Having spent considerable time preparing your ceremony, the rehearsal provides an opportunity to experience in advance, some of the joy which you will feel on the day itself.

If your ceremony is to be held outdoors, the rehearsal provides an opportunity to have a close look at the weather forecast and to decide together whether or not to proceed with an outdoor venue, or to advise guests of the alternate indoor venue. Sometimes indoor venues are alongside or nearby outdoor venues, and a decision can be made on the actual day in light of weather conditions.

15. Some other considerations

- Traditionally, the bride and groom don't see each other on the day of the wedding until the ceremony. This creates a heightened "impact" for both wedding partners at the commencement of the wedding ceremony.

- For a church wedding, relatives are provided with seats at the front. Traditionally, when viewed from the perspective of facing forward to where the bridal party are to stand, the bride's family sit to the left and the groom's family sit to the right.

- Always check whether or not it is acceptable to have people throw confetti. The mess it causes, and the difficulty in cleaning up, tend to mean most places prefer not to have confetti on the premises.

- It is advisable to attend to matters such as banking arrangements and insurances prior to actually getting married. You will need at some stage to decide on whether you will continue to operate separate bank accounts, or whether you will operate joint accounts, or both.

- Don't forget to arrange insurance cover for your anticipated wedding gifts.

- Finally, don't leave your honeymoon plans until the last minute. Make early reservations; arrange passports if required. Make sure, when the time comes, that you can get away from everybody and be together, on your own, where you want to be, for as long as possible.

3 — The marriage ceremony: structure and plan

We come now to the focus of your wedding day, and the heart of this book – the marriage ceremony. The chief point to be made about today's marriage ceremonies is this: just about anything goes. The main criterion for what happens, what is said, and by whom, is that it should all make sense and be meaningful to you. In other words, it is to be hoped that each couple will ensure that the ceremony by which their relationship is publicly acknowledged and legally constituted is as meaningful and appropriate to their own beliefs and situation as possible.

Many people say they cannot recall what was said at their wedding. They just went along with what they were told they had to say, without any real choice in the matter. Others recount the weddings they attended where they felt that the couple were merely going through religious or legal motions in order to be married. What was missing in all these occasions was the personal celebratory dimension. Creating your own marriage ceremony will result in precious memories which will last a life-time, not only for you, but for everyone who attends. The plan is to create a ceremony which "rings true" for you both.

Marriage is a relationship. The ceremony by which two people are married needs to be a ceremony that in fact celebrates the relationship. Whether a couple have been living together or not, they are already in a relationship together. At their wedding they are making a particular declaration on the nature of, and commitment to, this relationship. If the ceremony does not speak the language of the people involved, how can it in any sense celebrate their relationship? The shift in legal terminology from calling clergy "officiating ministers" to calling them "marriage celebrants" that occurred in New Zealand some years ago reflected more than just the fact that they were no longer the only ones licensed to perform weddings. They could just as easily have been called "marriage officiants." Celebration is the key ingredient.

While the reality of the legal contract of marriage is not overlooked, the primary focus is on making the sincerity of your relationship, public. Although there is an official requirement to establish a legal contract, this takes place within the context of a public celebration of your love for each other. So then, when it comes to celebrating your marriage, the choice is yours.

The law has no requirements regarding the format of the marriage ceremony, other than that each of the couple must say to the other: "I ...., take you ...., to be my legal husband (or wife)" – or utter words to similar effect. In other words, apart from the signing of the register, the law requires only the utterance of a minimal vow for the sake of legality.

Churches and religious groups have their own forms of wedding service. These have varying degrees of religious content because they are expressing a religious understanding of what marriage is about. Marriage celebrants who are not church or faith community leaders may also have a set ceremony. However, many celebrants, whether clergy or independent civil celebrants, are open to the option of helping a couple prepare their own unique ceremony. They may stipulate some minimal requirements of their own, but they are usually prepared to work with a couple so that the ceremony is personalised for and by the couple.

Within a broad framework that divides the typical marriage ceremony into three parts there is opportunity for maximum flexibility of content and expression. Always there is the extra option of "write your own," which may take the form of editing or amalgamating the words of two or more options in order to create a new one. Or you can simply write something completely fresh. Some elements could be omitted altogether, and the order of many of the component sections may be changed. But fundamentally you need a beginning, a middle and an end. That is the basis for our division of the ceremony into three sections that we have named 'setting the scene;' 'the main action;' and 'drawing to a close'. Within these you will find the numbered list of items that comprise a ceremony (although not all are necessarily used), and within each item there are a number of options. So, Sections and items provide the structure; the items give the content.

A summary of the options is found on page 41 and page 112. You can record your selections on page 112.

If you are accessing the electronic version of this book, you can copy and paste items to create a ceremony that can be modified as you wish. You can purchase eBook editions of the whole book, and access free downloadable checklists and summaries, on the publisher's website:

https://pgpl.co.nz/

The marriage ceremony is your ceremony. It's your wedding, so make it yours. Make your choice of options in accordance with what feels right for you. By choosing from among the options given, or by rewriting any or all of the sections to suit your own situation, you will have personalised the ceremony. Instead of a formal legal act alone, or a superficially meaningless religious ceremony, we encourage you to create a service which represents a real celebration of your unique relationship, a genuine act of commitment, a sincere expression of your own identities, inner feelings, spiritualities, faith/s, worldviews, hopes and understandings, in a language and form that rings true for you.

For more options, you may like to consult Michael Foley's book, *Wedding Rites* (2008), which contains a complete guide to traditional vows, music, ceremonies, blessings and interfaith services for Jewish, Catholic Christian and Protestant Christian couples. Also, *The Alternative Wedding Book*, which is published by Northstone (1996), provides many helpful suggestions and ideas. Details of these, and other resources are included in the Reference list at the end of this book.

Multi-choice marriage ceremony

Basic structure and item options

Section I – Setting the scene

    Item 1. Introduction 1 – 9

    Item 2. Prayer 1 – 6

    Item 3. Reading 1 – 12

Section II – The main action

    Item 4. Declaration of intention 1 – 7

    Item 5. The giving and affirmation 1 – 5

    Item 6. The vows 1 – 10

    Item 7. The rings 1 – 5

    Item 8. The pronouncement 1 – 6

Section III – Drawing to a close

    Item 9. Readings on love 1 – 9

    Item 10. Conclusion 1 – 7

    Item 11. The dismissal 1 – 5

    Item 12. The blessing 1 – 5

Together with the signing of the register – usually after item 8, or 9, or 10.

    Note: regarding song(s) or hymn(s):

If there is only one, then we suggest placing it somewhere in Section I; if two or more, then have them in Section I and III. See Appendix 1 for music options. Words for your song(s) or hymn(s) can be printed on your ceremony sheet or projected onto a screen.

Section I – Setting the scene

This first section, which sets the scene for the central part of your ceremony, contains three items: words of introduction, a prayer, and a reading.

If you wish to have a song or hymn that all your guests sing, then it is usually included here. A song near the beginning gives some "breathing space" to the bridal party. It can help settle nerves and generally ease the sense of tension that many couples, and sometimes their attendants, understandably feel once the big moment arrives.

In the following pages you will find a selection of introductions, prayers and readings from a variety of sources. For some, a reading takes the place of a song or hymn. But with or without singing, a reading can help set the scene for the "marriage act proper" that constitutes Section II.

If you would like your celebrant, minister, priest, pastor or priest (or friend or family member) to share a brief and relevant reflection during your ceremony, this is best incorporated at the end of Section 1. If you choose this option, ensure that the person given this responsibility does not intend to speak for too long. Around ten minutes is the suggested maximum for any message shared during a wedding ceremony.

Item 1: Introduction

Option 1:

> *Celebrant*:
>
> We have come together to witness the marriage of .... and ....
>
> We share with them in their happiness and their hopes for the future.
>
> Marriage is the most important and sacred commitment that two people can make to each other. .... and .... are about to make this commitment based on their mutual love and understanding.

In marriage two people become one. Marriage is not the domination of one by the other, but exists for the benefit of both.

Marriage enables two people to share their desires, longings, dreams and memories, and to help each other through their uncertainties. It provides the support and the encouragement to risk more and thus to gain more.

In marriage we learn to give each other reassurance by the complete sharing of ourselves – physically, emotionally, intellectually and spiritually.

Option 2:

Celebrant:

Friends and family of .... and ...., welcome. We have come to witness .... and .... give themselves to one another in marriage.

Marriage is the free association of a man and a woman (or: of two people) who love one another, who trust one another's love, and who want to share the future together.

Marriage provides security, stability and interdependence for husband and wife (or: the marriage partners). It provides for a secure and caring environment in which children can grow. It calls for a preparedness to give and take, a willingness to forgive and to be forgiven. Furthermore, marriage signifies a relationship and commitment recognised by society: a relationship of mutual trust and a commitment to family life.

This ceremony marks a starting point, a new beginning in a relationship that has already been established.

.... and .... are proclaiming to each other, to us who witness, and to society at large, their intentions and commitment to the future of their relationship.

Option 3:

Celebrant:

Friends and family of .... and ...., we have gathered to share in the marriage of these two people.

Marriage is the touching and flowing together of two life-streams, the joining together of two strands in the web of the universe.

We all partake of life, and the love we hold for each other reflects the love we have for humanity. Such love and respect is the most important thing in human relationships, not least in marriage. With it and by it we complete and fulfil each other.

Marriage provides the context for mutual flourishing and for a loving relationship to develop and grow. It calls for a capacity to both give and take, to forgive and be forgiven. It provides the opportunity for mutual support and sharing, the encouragement to risk and the chance to gain.

In choosing to weave their lives together in the relationship of marriage .... and .... are making the most important and sacred commitment that two people can make to each other.

Option 4:

Celebrant:

We have gathered so that .... and .... may be married.

Marriage means a man and a woman (or: two persons) living together faithfully, and loving one another throughout their lives.

Marriage means that each partner may help and support the other in every area of life. Marriage means the sharing together of joys as well as sorrows. Marriage enables a growing together in a closer and richer bond of love. Marriage is a communion of souls.

Within a healthy marriage relationship, children can experience love and acceptance from both parents, be properly cared for, and be guided toward truth and beauty and the valuing of human relationships.

Therefore, entering into marriage is a very significant act which should not be entered into thoughtlessly or light-heartedly. Marriage requires consistent sincerity, honesty and mutual respect. It requires also the ability to give and take and the willingness both to forgive, and to receive forgiveness. Ideally, marriage partners will grow closer and closer together in love and truth, throughout their lives.

It is in this spirit that .... and .... are to be married today.

Option 5:

Celebrant:

We have gathered here today so that .... and .... may marry each other.

Marriage involves making a commitment to developing and maintaining co-operation, friendship, and above all, mutual respect. Marriage means trust, understanding, honesty, patience, humour and lots of encouragement. Marriage means each partner cares for the other, and supports them in what they do.

Marriage demands courage of each partner – the courage to be open, the courage to grow and change, the courage to sort out and share together the tasks of everyday living.

Marriage requires closeness and distance – closeness for the couple growing together, and enough distance for each partner to be an individual. The poet Rilke has said: "A good marriage is one in which each partner appoints the other the guardian of their solitude." A good partner in such a marriage will also be a good parent, a good friend and a good worker.

We have also come together so that .... and .... may publicly make vows to each other.

.... and ...., we rejoice with you today. We are glad to join with you in the celebration of your marriage, to witness your vows, and support you in your intentions for your future life together.

Option 6:

Celebrant:

We are here in the name of Jesus Christ to witness and celebrate the marriage of .... and .... Marriage is a gift of God in creation. Marriage is not self-seeking but self-giving. It is the giving of each one to the other. It is an overcoming of separateness. The two become one.

Marriage is a creative relationship, blessed and sustained by God, who intends that husband and wife (or: each partner in marriage) should love and strengthen each other in good times and in bad.

A creative marriage has its place in the whole creative purpose of God. In Scripture it is recorded:

> "God created human beings, making them to be like himself. He created them male and female."
>
> *Genesis 1:27*

The Gospel according to Mark records these words of Jesus:

> "In the beginning, at the time of creation, 'God made them male and female,' as the scripture says. 'And for that reason a man will leave his father and mother and unite with his wife, and the two will become one.'"
>
> *Mark 10:6-7*

In marriage, husband and wife (or: each marriage partner) freely undertakes to share life together, while respecting each other as persons. It is a relationship through which the grace of God may flow into their lives and into the lives of others.

Marriage provides a secure foundation for home and family in which parents and children may grow in love and in the service of God and their fellows.

Marriage is therefore not to be undertaken lightly or ill-advisedly, but reverently and seriously. Marriage involves a serious and lifelong commitment in mutual love and joy to seek each other's good in a union of strength, sympathy and delight.

Marriage involves caring and giving. It involves learning to share one's life with another person. Forgiving as Christ forgives; enjoying the love and meaning which can be found together. It involves facing together whatever adversity may arise. It is to announce their commitment to this holy, creative relationship that .... and .... have come here today.

To the couple:

.... and ...., we rejoice with you; we are glad to join with you in the celebration of your marriage: to witness your vows, to pray with you; and to wish you joy in your life together.

Option 7:

Celebrant:

Welcome! We have come together in the presence of God to witness and celebrate the marriage of .... and .... The relationship of marriage is part of the divine plan for God's children. We are created in God's own image as male and female, for relational fulfilment. It is in God's purpose for love that we are drawn to each other. In Christian marriage husband and wife (or: each marriage partner) freely undertake/s to share life together and to respect each other as individual persons.

Marriage involves caring and giving. It involves forgiving as Christ forgives. It involves facing together whatever adversity may arise, and enjoying the love and meaning which can be found together. God intends that husband and wife (or: each marriage partner) should be united in heart, body and mind, and find in their union the fulfilment of their love for each other, and the stability necessary for family life and the care of children. Marriage, therefore, involves a serious and lifelong commitment in mutual love and joy under the grace and guidance of God.

.... and ...., we rejoice with you; we are glad to join with you in the celebration of your marriage: to witness your vows, to pray with you, and to wish you every joy and blessing in your life together.

Option 8:

Same-sex option.

[Options 1-7 above can also be used for same-sex ceremonies].

Celebrant:

Friends, we gather today (in the presence of God) to witness the marriage of .... and ...., to surround them with our loving support and to share in their joy.

or

Friends, we are here to witness and celebrate the marriage of .... and .... In gathering together today we gather surround them with loving support as we share in their joy. Today as .... and .... commit their lives in love to each other, let us commit ourselves to love and support them (and so celebrate God's love for us all.)

Option 9:

Māori language option:

Te Minita / Celebrant:

Nei te karanga a te Atua ki te whānau o tā tātou puhi māreikura. Mauria mai tā tātou tamāhine kia honoa ai ia ki te hono a te Atua, e kore nei e wewete e te tangata.

Ka haria mai a (Bride's name) ki te mahau e tōna matua.

Ka tangohia tana korowai ka whakahokia ki tōna matua.

(The Bride is brought forward and takes her place. If the Bride is wearing a Korowai it can be taken off here and given to her parents.)

E oku hoa aroha, e ngā whanaunga, ngā mana, ngā reo kei waenganui i a tātou i tēnei rā. Nau mai, haere mai ki tēnei honoa, tēnei mārena a .... rāua ko ....

Item 2: Prayer

Option 1:

Celebrant:

Let us give thanks for this marriage: Let us pray.

Loving God, we give thanks for the opportunity to come together today to share in this joyful and very significant ceremony.

Today we gather to celebrate and rejoice in the loving relationship of .... and ....

We give thanks for the love which has brought them together and which gives direction and purpose to their future.

We pray that in their life together .... and .... will come to know the depths of true love, and the blessing of true caring support of each other.

Grant them, we pray, the strength and grace to live and grow in each other's love. Amen.

Option 2:

Celebrant:

Let us give thanks for this marriage: Let us pray.

Almighty God, we thank you for the gift of marriage, for all the joys it can bring, for the promises it holds for a life of mutual concern and care.

We thank you that we can share in this joyful ceremony today.

We thank you for the love which has brought .... and .... together and on which they base their commitment to each other.

O God of all truth and love, we ask that you help and guide .... and .... as they enter their marriage. May they ever be as conscious of your concern and love for them as they are of each other's. May they ever be ready to give, and forgive, one to the other. May your love provide a pattern, and a source of strength, for their love in the years to come.

In the name of Jesus Christ,

Amen.

Option 3:

Celebrant:

.... and ...., before you take your vows, we want to wish you the richest blessings that marriage can bring. So, let us ask for a blessing on this marriage. Let us pray.

Creator of all, we are grateful for all that is important and precious in life. In particular, we are glad that .... and .... have decided to commit themselves to one another within the context of the marriage relationship.

Love is of the essence of life, and marriage provides a secure basis for love to develop and grow. We pray that the love .... and .... have for each other will never die, but deepen and increase as time goes by. May their love and care for each other last a lifetime. May their commitment to each other today in marriage, deepen their commitment to honest and open communication, and to deep and meaningful sharing, for the rest of their lives.

May their example of love be that of Jesus Christ who has shown us the meaning of loving acceptance and sacrificial service.

Amen.

Option 4:

Celebrant:

O God, Mother and Father to us all, bless us today with a sense of your presence as we gather together. Awaken us, we pray, to the wonder of life in all its fullness. Activate in us a spirit of love and care, both for those close to us, and for strangers.

Especially we ask your blessing on .... and .... who have freely chosen to come here to be married today. Inspire them as they make their promises to each other, that they may exchange their vows with deep sincerity. Renew in us all we pray, a heightened sense of joy, love and peace as a result of sharing in this sacred time.

Amen.

Option 5:

Same-sex option.

[Options 1-4 above can also be used for same-sex ceremonies]

Celebrant:

Gracious God, your generous love surrounds us, and everything we enjoy comes from you. In your great love you have given us the gift of marriage. Bless .... and .... as they pledge their lives to each other; that their love may continue to grow and be the true reflection of your love for us all; through Jesus Christ our Lord. Amen.

Option 6:

Māori language option.

Celebrant:

Nō reira kia timatahia tēnei karakia i runga i te ingoa a Te Matua, a Te Tama, a Te Wairua Tapu. Amine.

Kia inoi tātou:

E Te Atua Kaha rawa, E whakapaingia nei ake ake, e tuohu ana mātou ki tou aroaro i tēnei rā. E whakawhetai ana mātou ki a koe e te Atua mō tēnei rā tino ātaahua, kia whakatata mai koe ki a mātou e Te Hēpara Pai.

Manaakitia te kaupapa a tēnei rā, a tēnei karakia e te Atua, he tohu o tou aroha ki a mātou, he tohu o te aroha kei waenganui o ēnei tokorua. Ko Ihu Karakia hoki tō mātou Ariki. Amine.

Item 3: Reading

To be read by the Celebrant or another person chosen by the Marriage partners.

Option 1:

Go placidly amid the noise and haste, and remember what peace there may be in silence. As far as possible without surrender be on good terms with all persons. Speak your truth quietly and clearly; and listen to others.

If you compare yourself with others, you may become vain and bitter; for always there will be greater and lesser persons than yourself. Enjoy your achievements as well as your plans.

Be yourself. Especially, do not feign affection. Neither be cynical about love; for in the face of all aridity and disenchantment it is perennial as the grass.

Take kindly the counsel of the years, gracefully surrendering the things of youth. Nurture strength of spirit to shield you in sudden misfortune. But do not distress yourself with imaginings. Many fears are born of fatigue and loneliness. Beyond a wholesome discipline, be gentle with yourself.

Be at peace with God, whatever you conceive God to be, and whatever your labours and aspirations, in the noisy confusion of life keep peace with your soul.

With all its sham, drudgery and broken dreams, it is still a beautiful world. Be careful. Strive to be happy.

Desiderata (Abridged)
Found in Old Saint Paul's Church,
Baltimore, U.S.A.; Dated 1692

Option 2:

Go placidly amid the noise and haste,
And remember what peace there may be in silence.
Be yourself, especially do not feign affection.
Neither be cynical about love
For in the face of all aridity and disenchantment
It is perennial as the grass.
Be gentle with yourselves.
You are the children of the universe
No less than the trees and the stars.
Be at peace with God
Whatever you conceive God to be,
And whatever your labours and aspirations
In the noisy confusion of life
Keep peace with your souls.

Desiderata (selected lines)

Option 3:

Taking time to love
is what it's all about
what makes the clocks turn
and the sunsets come
true and without
complication

That doesn't mean
lying close
in shut-up rooms
or staying always
face to face

It's meant to cover walking,
being apart and knowing
that coming back together
makes small distances
even smaller

And taking the time
to love
is, most of all,
caring enough
to not hold on too tightly
and yet not run too loose.

'Taking the Time' Rod McKuen

Option 4:

Your friend is your needs answered,
S/He is your field which you sow with love,
and reap with thanksgiving
And s/he is your board and your fireside
For you come to her/him with your hunger,
and you seek your friend for peace.

When your friend speaks his/her mind,
you fear not the 'nay' in your own mind,
Nor do you withhold the 'aye'
And when your friend is silent,
your heart ceases not to listen to his/her heart
For without words, in friendship, all thoughts, all desires,
all expectations are born and shared,
with a joy that is unacclaimed,
When you are apart from your friend, you grieve not;
For that which you love most in her/him may be clearer
in her/his absence, as the mountain to the climber is
clearer from the plain.

And let your best be for your friend
If s/he must know the ebb of your tide,
let him/her know its flood also,
For what is your friend that you should seek her/him with
hours to kill?

Seek your friend always with hours to live
For it is his/hers to fill your need, but not your emptiness
And in the sweetness of friendship let there be laughter,
and sharing of pleasures
For in a dew of little things, the heart finds its morning
and is refreshed.

'Your Friend' Kahlil Gibran, adapted

Option 5:

A friend
is not afraid to see a person as they really are
what a friend sees does not bring judgement or a desire to end the friendship

A friend
can peek into the window of someone's soul and see
where they need the lifting the strengthening and the loving.

Anon

Option 6:

If two are caring, as they're sharing life's hopes and fears,
if the music of laughter outweighs sadness of tears,
Marriage is togetherness.

If both derive pleasure from mere presence of each other,
Yet when parted no jealousies restrict, worry or smother,
Marriage is freedom.

If achievements mean more when they benefit two
And consideration is shown with each point of view,
Marriage is respect.

And if togetherness, freedom and respect are combined
With a joy that words can never fully define,
Then marriage is love.

'Marriage is Love' Gloria Matthews

Option 7:

You and I are in a relationship which I value and want to keep. Yet each of us is a separate person with our own needs and the right to meet those needs.

When you are having problems meeting your needs, I will try to really listen to you and let you find your own answers instead of depending on mine. I will really try to respect your right to choose your own beliefs and develop your own values – even if they are different from mine!

However, when your behaviour interferes with what I must do to get my own needs met, I will tell you openly and honestly how your behaviour affects me, trusting that you respect my needs and feelings enough to try to change the behaviour that is unacceptable to me. Also, whenever some behaviour of mine is unacceptable to you, I hope you will tell me openly and honestly so I can try to change my behaviour.

At those times when we find that either of us cannot change to meet the other's needs, let us acknowledge that we have a conflict and commit ourselves to receive each such conflict without either of us resorting to the use of power or authority to win at the expense of the other's losing. I respect your needs, but I also must respect my own. So let us always look for a solution that will be acceptable to both of us. Your needs will be met, and so will mine – neither will lose, both will win.

In this way, you can continue to develop as a person through satisfying your needs, and so can I. Then ours can be a healthy relationship in which both of us can strive to become what we are capable of being. And we can continue to relate to each other with mutual respect, love and peace.

Marriage, a Credo. Anon.

Option 8:

> A person's struggle for significance
> apart from God's will and purposes is in vain.
>
> We build homes and institutions;
> we acquire property and possessions;
> we crowd the cities with the clutter
> of questionable achievements;
> we fill the better part of every day
> with self-centered activities;
> we push and prod in an anxiety-ridden quest
> for some ephemeral treasure;
> we strive incessantly to get to the top.
>
> And all the while worth and value are within us
> or very close to us.
> They are the precious gifts of God
> that come in some measure to each of us.
> There are visible signs of a person's worth:
> the beloved mate who brings us joy
> the children we beget
> the ability to supply our own and our family's needs
> through our daily labours.
>
> But even beyond this,
> and long before this,
> our true worth was established
> by the Lord our God.
>
> *Psalms 127 & 128 (paraphrase by Leslie Brandt)*

Option 9:

> You were born together,
> and together you shall be for evermore.
> You shall be together
> when the white wings of death scatter your days.
> Aye, you shall be together
> even in the silent memory of God.
> But let there be spaces in your togetherness.
> And let the winds of heaven dance between you.

Love one another, but make not a bond of love:
Let it rather be a moving sea
between the shores of your souls.
Fill each other's cup but drink not from one cup.
Give one another of your bread
but eat not from the same loaf.

Sing and dance together and be joyous,
but let each one of you be alone,
Even as the strings of a lute are alone
though they quiver with the same music.

Give your hearts, but not into each other's keeping.
For only the hand of Life can contain your hearts.

And stand together yet not too near together:
For the pillars of the temple stand apart,
And the oak tree and the cypress grow
not in each other's shadow.

Kahlil Gibran, from 'The Prophet'

Option 10:

Let me not to the marriage of true minds
Admit impediments. Love is not love
Which alters when it alteration finds,
Or bends with the remover to remove.

Oh no! It is an ever fixed mark,
That looks on tempests and is never shaken;
It is the star to every wandering bark,
Whose worth's unknown, although his height be taken.

Love's not time's fool, though rosy lips and cheeks
Within his bending sickle's compass come;
Love alters not with his brief hours and weeks,
But bears it out even to the edge of doom.

If this be error and upon me proved,
I never writ, nor no man ever loved.

William Shakespeare

Part One   Getting Married

Option 11:

> Out of the wild exuberance of creation
> throughout millions of years,
> you two have appeared –
> Each of you unique, distinctive, wondrously personal.
> You have chosen to journey together
> down this earth valley in the brief moment
> of time that is yours.
>
> From this day forward, you become a unit
> of life that will bring forth futures.
>
> You are both called into a new existence.
> The old things have passed away;
> a new heaven and a new earth is now
> your dwelling place.
>
> For the whole universe has come to each of you
> in the form of a particular person
> who has a unique love for you
> and is beloved by you.
>
> Ross Snyder, 'Inscape'

Option 12:

Māori language ceremony, or could be included in a bilingual ceremony.

> He manawanui te aroha, ā, he atawhai;
> E kore te aroha e hae; e kore te aroha e whakahīhī,
> e kore e whakapehapeha
> Kāhore ōna tikanga whānoke, e kore e whai ki āna ake.
> E kore e riri wawe, e kore e whakairi kino;
> E kore e hari ki te hē, engari ka hari tahi me te pono
> E whakamanawanui ana ki ngā mea katoa,
> E whakapono ana ki ngā mea katoa
> E tūmanako ana ki ngā mea katoa
> E whakaririka kau ana ki ngā mea katoa.
>
> I Koroniti 13:4-7 (1 Corinthians 12: 4-7)

Further readings suitable for wedding ceremonies can be found online or in the excellent New Zealand resource, *Heartsongs* –

readings for weddings by P. Agnew (2004). See Appendix 3: Reference list for details.

Section II – The main action

This middle part of your ceremony forms the "act of marriage," the main action of your ceremony. This is where you commit your lives to each other through the sharing of carefully prepared sincere vows, and the giving and receiving of rings.

Item 4 is a public declaration of intention put in the form of a question to which the couple respond in the affirmative, saying, "I will" or "We will."

Item 5, the "giving and/or affirmation" provides an opportunity for family and friends to express their support for the couple, not only on the day of the ceremony, but also on into the future.

Item 6 the centre point of the whole ceremony, contains options for your vows. We provide the traditional "I take" type of vow; vows that use "give and take" language; vows that state a simple promise; vows that begin with the simple words "I love you;" and a vow that acknowledges the context of the already established living-together relationship.

If one of these vows doesn't say it for you, then write your own. Let the vow you make to each other be an expression from the depth of your being, something which says. "Here I stand; I stand with you." The vows you make together will set the tone for the ongoing development of your relationship. You do not have to say a lot, it can be very simple. Only let it be utterly real and sincere for you. But do not forget that your vow is a public statement. Be thoughtful and careful therefore in your choice of expression. Legally, you are required to state your name, the name of your partner, and to make it clear that your vow is a marriage vow, by including the word marriage.

Item 7 provides options for words to be used in respect of sealing the vows made with the gift of a ring. Where there are two rings, special words are spoken as you place a ring on each other's "ring finger," the third finger on your left hand. If you choose to have only one ring, only one of you need say the words provided. Sometimes people do not wish to have any ring, in which case an alternative "token" might be given or exchanged. The point of the ring, or tokens, is to function as a symbol of the vows and all that is intended and hoped for when you share them with each other.

Item 8 offers a selection of pronouncements for the celebrant to declare that you are now, in fact married. Opinions vary regarding when, precisely, a couple are actually married. Some say at the point they make their vows. Others say not until the marriage register has been signed by all parties. Still others claim it is when the celebrant declares them to be married. The answer will depend upon whether you as a couple view your marriage commitment as primarily a spiritual/religious or a legal commitment. We believe it to be both!

The signing of the register can take place at any time after the exchange of ring(s), i.e. Item 7, and before the dismissal (Item 11). There is some sense in having it before Item 8, but it can just as easily be left till later.

Item 4: Declaration of Intention

Note: the wording in all of these options can be modified for same-sex ceremonies, simply by substituting "partner" or "spouse" for "Groom" and "Bride." However, we acknowledge that many same-sex partners choose to use these traditional terms. Pronouns "him/her" will also need to be changed to "him/him" or "her/her" when adapting the material here for same-sex ceremonies.

Option 1:

Celebrant to Groom:

…………, will you have ………… to be your wife? Will you love her, comfort her, honour and keep her, in sickness and in health, remaining faithful to her as long as you both shall live?

Groom: I will.

Celebrant to Bride:

............, will you have .... to be your husband? Will you love him, comfort him, honour and keep him, in sickness and in health, remaining faithful to him as long as you both shall live?

Bride: I will.

Option 2

Celebrant to Groom:

............, do you love and trust ...., and want to give yourself to be her husband, to live together sharing all things?

Groom: Yes, I do.

Celebrant:

Will you stand by her, respecting her individuality, understanding her needs, accepting her and enjoying her love forever?

Groom: I will.

Celebrant to Bride:

............, do you love and trust............, and want to give yourself to be his wife, to live together sharing all things?

Bride: Yes, I do.

Celebrant:

Will you stand by him, respecting his individuality, understanding his needs, accepting him and enjoying his love forever?

Bride: I will.

Option 3:

Celebrant to Groom:

............, sharing with .... a relationship of love, tenderness, and laughter, will you stand by her through all her tomorrows, respecting her as a person, her individuality, her needs, her changes, and enjoying her love through all your life together?

Groom: I will.

Celebrant to Bride:

............, sharing with .... a relationship of love, tenderness, and laughter, will you stand by him through all his tomorrows, respecting him as a person, his individuality, his needs, his changes, and enjoying his love through all your life together?

Bride: I will.

Option 4:

Celebrant to Groom and Bride, or partners in Marriage:

.... and ...., have you come here freely and without reservation to give yourselves to each other in marriage?

Bride and Groom, or partners in marriage: We have.

Celebrant:

Will you love, honour, and respect each other as husband and wife (or: partners in marriage)?

Bride and Groom, or partners in marriage: We will.

Option 5:

Celebrant to Groom and Bride, or partners in marriage:

.... and ...., are you here of your own free will, without question, to give of yourselves to each other in marriage, to love and honour each other and any children you may raise, seeking to do your best to bring them to know the love of God?

Bride and Groom, or partners in marriage: We are.

Option 6:

Same sex ceremony option.

> *The Celebrant addresses each of the couple in turn*:
>
>> ...., do you freely and unreservedly offer yourself to ....?
>
> *Answer*: I do.
>
> *Celebrant*:
>
>> Will you live together in faithfulness and holiness of life as long as you both shall live?
>
> *Answer*: I will.

Option 7:

Māori language or bilingual service option.

> *Note*: This is a statement about the meaning of marriage, spoken by the minister / celebrant. See Part Five for a full Māori language ceremony.
>
> *Celebrant*:
>
>> Atu i tēnei wā, me aro kōrua ki a kōrua, kia noho kōrua hei hoa pūmau kōrua mō ake tonu atu. Kia kaha tā kōrua whakahōnore, whakatenatena, tautoko anō a tētahi i tētahi. I ngā wā o te taumahatanga, mā kōrua anō kōrua e hāpai kia tutuki rawa ai i tā kōrua mārena tētahi āhua kihai i taea e te kotahi. Manaakitia tō kōrua aroha, ā, tohea ko tā kōrua hono hei hono tātai e kore e oti noa. I te pātukitanga o te manawa, me aroha kōrua ki a kōrua – tētahi ki tētahi.

Item 5: The Giving and Affirmation

Option 1:

> *Celebrant*:
>
>> Who gives this woman to be married?
>
> *Respondent* (traditionally the father of the bride): I do.

Option 2:

Celebrant:

Parents, by their presence, are saying to .... and .... that they pledge their loving support.

Do you, the parents of .... and ...., give them to be married?

Parents: We do.

Option 3:

Celebrant:

Do you, the parents of .... and ...., give your blessing to their marriage and promise to do all you can to support them on into the future?

Parents: We do.

Option 4:

Celebrant:

(Parents/The Children of ..../Family members), by your presence here today, are showing your affirmation and support to .... and .... I would like to give you the opportunity now to make this support very clear, by asking you this question:

Do you, the (Parents/Children/Family) of .... and ...., affirm their marriage and promise to do all you can to support them in their marriage relationship on into the future? If so, please express your support by enthusiastically saying, "We do!"

Enthusiastic response from everyone: We do!

Option 5:

Celebrant:

> Will you, the families and friends of .... and ...., who have gathered to share in this wedding day, uphold them in their marriage on into the future?

Response from everyone: We will.

Item 6: The Vows

Note: the wording in all of these options can be modified for same-sex ceremonies by, for example, substituting "partner" or "spouse" for "Groom" and "Bride."

Option 1:

Groom:

> I, ..., take you ...., to be my wife, to have and to hold from this day forward, for better, for worse, for richer, for poorer, in sickness and in health, to love and to cherish, so long as we both shall live.

Bride:

> I, ..., take you ...., to be my husband, to have and to hold from this day forward, for better, for worse, for richer, for poorer, in sickness and in health, to love and to cherish, so long as we both shall live.

Option 2:

Groom:

> I love you.
>
> Before this gathering, and in accordance with the laws of this land, I, ..., take you, ..., to be my legal wife.

Bride:

> I love you.

Before this gathering, and in accordance with the laws of this land, I, ..., take you, ..., to be my legal husband.

Option 3:

Groom:

............, in the presence of God, and before this gathering, I promise to be your true and faithful husband, to love and care for you always.

Bride:

............, in the presence of God, and before this gathering, I promise to be your true and faithful wife, to love and care for you always.

Option 4:

Groom:

I love you .... Today I take you to be my wife, and I give myself to be your husband. I shall value the good times we have together and give you help and support in any adversity. I shall love and cherish you always.

Bride:

I love you .... Today I take you to be my husband, and I give myself to be your wife. I shall value the good times we have together and give you help and support in any adversity. I shall love and cherish you always.

Option 5:

Groom:

............, I have lived with you and I love you. Today I give myself to be your husband, and I take you to be my wife. Whatever life may bring, I will love you and care for you always.

Bride:

> ...., I have lived with you and I love you. Today I give myself to be your wife, and I take you to be my husband. Whatever life may bring, I will love you and care for you always.

Option 6:

Groom:

> I love you .... Today I give myself to be your husband and I take you to be my wife. Whatever life may bring I will love you and care for you always.

Bride:

> I love you .... Today I give myself to be your wife and I take you to be my husband. Whatever life may bring I will love you and care for you always.

Option 7:

Groom:

> I call upon all here present to witness that I, ..., take you ...., to be my lawful wedded wife. I will love you, trust you, believe in you as you are, be honest with you, encourage you, support you in your endeavours, care for you and above all else, respect you as a person of equal worth, and with equal rights and responsibilities – in sickness as in health, for better for worse, through all our life together.

Bride:

> I call upon all here present to witness that I, ..., take you ...., to be my lawful wedded husband. I will love you, trust you, believe in you as you are, be honest with you, encourage you, support you in your endeavours, care for you and above all else, respect you as a person of equal worth, and with equal rights and responsibilities – in sickness as in health, for better for worse, through all our life together.

Option 8:

Groom: ...., I take you to be my wife.

Bride: ...., I take you to be my husband.

Together:

> To laugh with you in joy,
> To grieve with you in sorrow,
> To grow with you in love,
> To live with you in peace and hope,
> As long as we both shall live.

The bridegroom turns and faces the congregation and says:

> I ask everyone here to witness that I, ... receive .... to be my wife.

He then faces the bride, takes her hands, and says:

> ...., all that I am I give to you,
> and all that I have I share with you.

> Whatever the future holds,
> I will love you and strengthen you,
> As long as we both shall live.

> This is my solemn pledge.

The bride turns and faces the congregation, and says:

> I ask everyone here to witness that I .... receive .... to be my husband.

She then faces the bridegroom, takes his hand, and says:

> ...., all that I am I give to you,
> and all that I have I share with you.

> Whatever the future holds,
> I will love and strengthen you,
> As long as we both shall live.

> This is my solemn pledge.

Option 9:

Same-sex ceremony option.

> I, ..., in the presence of God
> take you, ..., to be my marriage partner/husband/wife;
> to have and to hold,
> from this day forward,
> for better, for worse,
> for richer, for poorer,
> in sickness and in health,
> to love and to cherish,
> as long as we both shall live.
> This is my solemn vow.

Option 10:

Māori or bilingual ceremony option.

> *Celebrant to the Groom:*

> Ki Te Tane: Ka hono atu koe ki a .... hei wahine pūmau mōhou
> Kia arohaina atu, kia whakahōnoretia e koe
> I te wā o te mate, o te ora rānei
> I ngā wā o te pai, o te kino rānei
> Atu i tēnei rā, ā tutuki noa

Groom: Ae!

Celebrant to the Bride:

> Ki Te Wahine: Ka hono atu koe ki a .... hei wahine pūmau mōhou
> Kia arohaina atu, kia whakahōnoretia e koe
> I te wā o te mate, o te ora rānei
> I ngā wā o te pai, o te kino rānei
> Atu i tēnei rā, ā tutuki noa

Bride: Ae!

Ngā Oati Tapu (Sacred vows/oaths)

Te Tāne / Groom:

> E tono atu nei au ki a koutou katoa,
> kia mātakihia mai koutou, e hono atu nei ahau ....
> i a .... hei wahine pūmau mōku

Te Wahine / Bride responds:

> Ko tōku katoa ka tuku nei ki a koe
> ko aku rawa katoa ka hoatu ki a koe.
> Ahakoa te aha, ka aroha ahau ki a koe, kia tū tahi ai tāua,
> ā tutuki noa, ko taku oati tēnei ka hoatu ki a koe

Te Wahine / Bride:

> E tono atu nei au ki a koutou katoa
>
> kia mātakihia mai koutou, e hono atu nei ahau ....
> i a .... hei tāne pūmau mōku

Te Tāne / Groom responds:

> Ko tōku katoa ka tuku nei ki a koe
> ko aku rawa katoa ka hoatu ki a koe.
> Ahakoa te aha, ka aroha ahau ki a koe, kia tū tahi ai tāua,
> ā tutuki noa, ko taku oati tēnei ka hoatu ki a koe

Item 7. The Exchange of Rings

Note: For same sex ceremonies, substitute "partner" and "spouse" for "Groom" and "Bride."

Option 1:

Celebrant:

> Let us pray. (*Holds rings*)
>
> Bless, O Lord, the giving of these rings. May .... and .... be ever faithful to each other, and continue to love so long as they both shall live, Amen.

Groom, then Bride:

> ...., I give you this ring in token of the vow made between us, and as a sign of my love and affection for you.

Option 2:

Celebrant:

> Wedding rings serve as a symbol of the vows you have just made. They are the outward and visible sign of an inward and invisible love which binds your lives together. As they are of the finest of earth's materials, so your love is of the richest of human values. As rings are without edge or seam, having no beginning and no end, they symbolise the perfection of love which knows no end.

Groom, then Bride:

> ...., this ring I give you, in token of our marriage vow. May it ever be a symbol of the unbroken bond of our love and of all that we share together.

Option 3:

Groom, then Bride:

> ...., I give this ring as a token of my love, and as evidence of the vow we have made together. May it forever signify the love we have for each other.

Option 4:

Groom, then Bride:

> ...., I give you this ring in token of the circle of affection and tenderness I will surround you with. Wear it as a symbol of all that we share together.

Option 5:

Māori language or bilingual ceremony.

Ngā Rīngi.

Ka waiho ngā ringi ki runga i te Paipera Tapu – the rings are placed on the Holy Bible.

The blessing of the rings by the Minister/ Celebrant:

Kia inoi tātou – kia whakapaingia ēnei rīngi hei tohu i te aroha o tētahi ki tētahi. He rite tonu ki tō te Atua aroha ki a tātou – kāore tōna timatanga, kāore tōna mutunga.

E te Matua, Tama, Wairua Tapu, anei ngā taonga o te aroha.

Whakatapua ēnei taonga o te aroha mō te painga o Ihu Karaiti, tō mātou Ariki

Amine.

The giving and receiving of rings:

Te Tāne / Groom:

.... ka hoatu nei au i tēnei rīngi ki a koe hei tohu i tō tāua aroha me ngā oati tapu kua whakapuakina ake i te rā nei

Te Wahine / Bride:

Ae, e tango nei au i tēnei rīngi, hei tohu i tō tāua aroha me ngā oati tapu kua whakapuakina ake i te rā nei

Te Wahine / Bride:

.... ka hoatu nei au i tēnei rīngi ki a koe hei tohu i tō tāua aroha me ngā oati tapu kua whakapuakina ake i te rā nei

Te Tāne / Groom:

Ae, e tango nei au i tēnei rīngi, hei tohu i tō tāua aroha me ngā oati tapu kua whakapuakina ake i te rā nei

Item 8: The Pronouncement

Option 1:

Celebrant:

.... and ...., you have freely expressed your desire to be united in marriage and have made vows to each other. Therefore, I pronounce you husband and wife (or: partners in marriage) in the name of the Father, and of the Son, and of the Holy Spirit. May God bless you and these rings which you have exchanged as a sign of your mutual love.

Option 2:

Celebrant:

.... and ...., you have made promises to each other, and as a symbol of these vows you have given and received a ring.

Let the world now recognise that you are now husband and wife together (or: partners in marriage). May you treasure this trust and responsibility; may no failure nor misfortune ever part you; and may you live full and rich lives together.

Option 3:

Celebrant:

.... and ...., you have made promises to each other and you have exchanged rings as a symbol of your love. I now pronounce you to be husband and wife (or: partners in marriage).

On behalf of all who are gathered here, I extend to you our good wishes, our friendship and love, in support of the commitment you have made to each other. May your love deepen and grow through all the trials and triumphs that life has to offer you.

Option 4:

Celebrant:

.... and ...., you are fulfilling the formalities required by custom and law to establish a relationship of marriage.

You have expressed the love and affection you have for each other, and signified your intentions for your future life.

You are aware that such a deep personal relationship is not easily attained. There will be times when it will seem so difficult that you will be tempted to give up. At such times, recall the earnestness and sincerity of the vows you have made today and find the strength to go on.

Remember our sharing with you as an expression of our desire to continue our friendship and concern in the days ahead. And there will be times in the development of your relationship that will bring you great joy, and we will be glad for you.

.... and ...., I now pronounce you husband and wife / (or: partners in marriage).

Option 5:

Celebrant:

.... and ...., you have made your promises one to the other before us all.

I now pronounce you to be husband and wife (or: partners in marriage), and express on behalf of us all our deep desire for your joy and happiness together.

Option 6:

Māori language or bilingual ceremony

Note: Te Whakatau takes place at the end of the ceremony, after the signing of the register / marriage certificate. This positioning of the declaration, affirms the significance of both spiritual and legal dimensions of marriage.

Te Whakatau: Declaration of Marriage by the Minister/Celebrant:

.... kōrua ko .... kua whakaaturia tō kōrua aroha
I mua i te aroaro o ō kōrua whānau me ō kōrua hoa
Kua whakapuakina mai he oati tapu
Ā, kua whakatinanahia ai tēnei mā te hono i ngā ringa me te tuku i ngā rīngi

Mā te mana kua ūhia nei au e te Hāhi me te Karauna
Māku anō kōrua e whakatau:

Hei Tāne, Hei Wahine Pūmau

Section III – Drawing to a close

The end or "rounding-off" section, which draws your ceremony to a close, should not be overlooked. You will want the occasion to finish on a good note. If you wish to have a second song or hymn, then this would be the place to insert it, sometime before Item 12, unless you choose to have everyone singing as you walk out. Also, if you haven't included the signing of the register in Section II, then it needs to take place somewhere during Section III. Again, details of the final order or sequence of events should be discussed with your marriage celebrant.

Item 9 contains some readings on love from the Bible, each prefaced by an introduction, plus additional "love" readings from other sources. There are a number of passages in Christian scripture pertaining to marriage. They seek to express principles and values that are both central to faith and expressive of values which are deeply significant for the development of a healthy marriage relationship. For example, honesty, sincerity and faithfulness. You do not have to be religious or an active church member to find in them an expression of an ideal, or a perspective which you would like to include in your ceremony.

Item 10 provides options for words of conclusion, including suitable final prayers along with statements of a reflective nature. The point of this section is to focus the thoughts of everyone on what has been said and done in the ceremony, and to wish the couple well as they move forward from that moment.

All that remains to be said are some words of dismissal (Item 11) and, if you wish it, a brief blessing (Item 12).

Item 9: Readings on love

May be read by the Celebrant or another person chosen by the Bride and Groom, or partners in marriage.

Option 1:

.... and .... are now married, but a marriage is never established in a brief moment of time. Rather it is built up over the years as two people grow together. More than that, it has to be worked at by the couple. In the process there are certain qualities to be cultivated that make for an enriching and lasting relationship. These have been expressed in the Christian tradition by the words of the Apostle Paul. His thoughts on love provide a sound foundation for the marriage relationship to grow and flourish. Listen to what he wrote:

Love is slow to lose patience – it looks for a way of being constructive. It is not possessive: it is neither anxious to impress nor does it cherish inflated ideas of its own importance.

Love has good manners and does not pursue selfish advantage. It is not touchy. It does not keep account of evil or gloat over the wickedness of other people. On the contrary it is glad ... when truth prevails.

Love knows no limit to its endurance, no end to its trust, no fading of its hope; it can outlast anything. It is, in fact, the one thing that still stands when all else has fallen.

In this life we have three great lasting qualities – faith, hope and love. But the greatest of them is love.

1 Corinthians 13:4-8 and 13
(J.B. Phillips translation)

Option 2:

.... and .... are now married, but this relationship is not established in a brief moment of time. Rather it has to be worked at. It deepens as two people grow together. It is tested by life's trials and storms. It is strengthened by the conscious cultivation of human spiritual values such as are expressed within the Christian tradition.

From the Old Testament, the book of Ruth, we find these words expressing personal commitment:

> "Entreat me not to leave you;
> Or to return from following you;
> For where you go, I will go;
> And where you lodge, I will lodge;
> And your God, my God."
>
> *Ruth 1:16-17*

From the New Testament, the letter to the Colossians, we find these words of loving advice:

> Put on, then, as God's chosen ones, holy and beloved, compassion, kindness, lowliness, meekness and patience, forbearing one another and, if one has a complaint against another, forgiving each other; as the Lord has forgiven you so you also must forgive. And above all these, put on love, which binds everything together in perfect harmony. And let the peace of Christ rule in your hearts.
>
> *Colossians 3:12-15*

Option 3:

.... and .... are now married, but a marriage is never established in a brief moment of time. It is a relationship that requires to be worked at. Its foundation and strength, is love. Love is the great spiritual quality of human existence. It is the reality that lies at the heart of faith.

Let us reflect on love as we hear these words from the New Testament, from the first letter of St John:

> Dear friends, let us love one another, because love comes from God. Whoever loves is a child of God and knows God. Whoever does not love does not know God, for God is love. And God showed his love for us by sending

his only Son into the world, so that we might have life through him. This is what love is: it is not that we have loved God, but that he loves us and sent his Son to be the means by which our sins are forgiven.

Dear friends, if this is how God loved us, then we should love one another. No one has ever seen God, but if we love one another, God lives in union with us, and his love is made perfect in us.

1 John 4:7-12

Option 4:

This passage gives expression to the physical attraction between a man and a woman.

The Groom may speak the first part:

> You have ravished my heart, my sister, my bride,
> You have ravished my heart with a glance of your eyes,
> with one jewel of your necklace.
>
> How sweet is your love, my sister, my bride,
> how much better is your love than wine,
> and the fragrance of your oils than any spice.
>
> Your lips distil nectar, my bride:
> honey and milk are under your tongue;
> the scent of your garments is like the scent of Lebanon.
>
> Set me as a seal upon your heart,
> as a seal upon your arm;
> for love is as strong as death.
> Many waters cannot quench love,
> neither can floods drown it.

The Bride may respond with the second part:

> As an apple tree among the trees of the wood,
> so is my beloved among young men.
>
> With great delight I sat in his shadow
> and his fruit was sweet to my taste.

He brought me to the banqueting house,
and his banner over me was love.

O that his left hand were under my head,
and that his right hand embraced me

I hear the voice of my beloved.
Behold he comes ...

My beloved is mine and I am his.

From 'The Song of Solomon'

Option 5:

.... and ...., this is a turning point today. Another turning point was that day you discovered you loved each other in a way never known before. And think today how your love has grown since that first day. Your lives have blossomed with each other – each of you helping the other strengthen and grow. And this day is like that first day – for growing people like you will never stop growing, but will look back on this day and smile, and love again the ways your love has grown. Together you will grow, bound gently by a love described so beautifully in *The Prophet* by Kahlil Gibran.

> Love one another, but make not a bond of love. Let it rather be a moving sea between the shores of your souls.
>
> Fill each other's cup, but drink not from one cup. Sing and dance together and be joyous, but let each of you be alone, even as the strings of the lute are alone, though they quiver with the sounds of the same music.
>
> Give your hearts, but not into each other's keeping. For only the hand of life can contain your hearts. And stand together, yet not too near together, for the pillars of the temple stand apart, and the oak tree and the cypress grow not in each other's shadow.

Option 6:

> Love gives naught but itself
> and takes naught but from itself.

Love possesses not nor would it be possessed;
For love is sufficient unto love.

And think not you can direct the course of love,
for love, if it finds you worthy, directs your course.

Love has no other desire but to fulfil itself.

But if you love and must needs have desires,
let these be your desires:

To melt and be like a running brook
that sings its melody to the night.

To know the pain of too much tenderness.

To be wounded by your own understanding of love;
And to bleed willingly and joyfully.

To wake at dawn with a winged heart
and give thanks for another day of loving;
To rest at the noon hour and meditate love's ecstasy;

To return home at eventide with gratitude;
And then to sleep with a prayer for the beloved in your
heart and a song of praise upon your lips.

Kahlil Gibran: The Prophet, 12-15

Option 7:

Love is sensing the other as a Presence.

This is now the mode of your existence.

Love is receiving the feelings, thoughts,
intentions of the other into your own understanding.

Love is fidelity over the long haul.

"Entreat me not to leave thee, ...
for wherever you go, I will go"
in the battle for excellence,
in the tension of differences,
in the travail of defeat,
in the joy of being warmly human.

Love is body infused with spirit ...
united in ecstasy with another whole person.

Love is talking together.

Love is listening together.

Love is creating together.

Ross Snyder: Inscape, 14-16 (adapted)

Option 8: An inclusive Eucharistic prayer

To be offered before the couple receive Holy Communion (another option.)

Holy mystery,
Energy that powers the Universe,
Your Word set creation into motion:
ever-expanding, evolving, multiplying, flourishing.

You brought human life out of primordial mist,
setting us in this garden home,
instilling in us the capacity to love,
endowing us with the imagination
to form friendships and make love.

We heard you tell our ancient parents
that it is not good to be alone
and command them to fill the earth with blessing.
Yet, so often, we were afraid.

We failed to nurture your good creation.
We limited the wideness of your love
by pretending that some are loved by you,
and others are outside your grace.

Again and again, you sent men to remind us of mercy,
and women to demand justice.

At the right time, you sent Jesus,
an open channel of light and love,
who turned water into wine,

rejection into welcome,
hunger into fullness,
and death into life.

*Kimberly Bracken Long: From this day forward –
rethinking the Christian wedding, pp.141-142
Kindle edition. Westminster John Knox Press*

Option 9:

Choose from this selection of appropriate Bible Readings. This is not an exhaustive list.

Old Testament

Psalm 67: May God be merciful to us and bless us

Psalm 100: Be joyful in the Lord, all you lands

Psalm 128: Happy are they all who fear the Lord

Song of Solomon 2:10-13; 8:6-7: Many waters cannot quench love

Epistle

1 Corinthians 13:1-13: Love is patient and kind

Ephesians 3:14-21: The Father, from whom every family is named

Colossians 3:12-17: Love which binds everything together

1 John 4:7-16: Let us love one another, for love is of God

Gospel

Matthew 5:1-10: The Beatitudes

Matthew 5:13-16: You are the light... let your light shine

Matthew 7:21-29: Hearing and doing

Matthew 22:35-40: This is the greatest and first commandment

John 2:1-11: The marriage at Cana in Galilee

John 15:1-8: Abide in me, and I in you

John 15:9-17: This I command you, to love one another

Item 10: Conclusion

Option 1:

Celebrant:

Let us pray.

Eternal God, we give thanks to you for creating humanity in the form of male and female so that each may find fulfilment in the other.

We praise you for all the ways in which love comes into our lives, and for all the joys that can come to men and women through marriage.

Today especially we think of .... and .... as they begin their new life together. With them we thank you for giving them life and for the love and care of their parents which has guided them to maturity and prepared them for each other. We pray also for their parents, that at this moment of parting they may find new happiness as they share their children's joy.

Give .... and .... strength, we pray, to keep the vows they have made, to be loyal and faithful to each other, and to support each other throughout their life. May they bear each other's burdens and share each other's joys. Help them to be honest and patient with each other, to be loving and wise parents of any children they may have, and to welcome both friends and strangers into their home.

In all their future together, may they enjoy each other's lives and grow in each other's love.

In the name of Jesus Christ Our Lord, Amen.

Option 2:

Celebrant:

Let us pray.

Almighty and Ever-loving God, we pray for .... and .... who have been joined together in marriage. Give them strength to keep the vows they have made. May they be loyal and faithful to each other, and be to one another a strength in need, a guide in difficulties, a comfort in sorrow, and a companion in joy.

May their lives be an example of your love in this world, so that unity may overcome estrangement, forgiveness may heal guilt, and hope triumph over despair.

May they grow in the love that they have expressed today.

Amen.

Option 3:

Celebrant:

Let us pray.

O Lord our God, we ask now that your blessing rest upon .... and .... Grant that they may live together always in unity and love.

May they always have patience in times of trouble and stress, faithful devotion for one another and a tender concern for each other's wants and needs.

May their love never die, rather may it deepen and increase so that they may be forever as they are now: happily in love, and glad to be married to each other.

Through Jesus Christ Our Lord, Amen.

Option 4:

Celebrant:

Let us spend a moment in silence as we reflect on the love that .... and .... share with each other. Let us remember that we also have received love, and that we all have love to give.

.... and ...., you have committed yourselves to one another in love, joy and tenderness. You stand on the threshold of an experience of relationship which can touch the richest meanings and deepest mysteries of human life.

We have shared this moment with you, and pray you will continue to grow in faith, hope and love.

Amen.

Option 5:

Celebrant:

Let us give thanks for the joy of this occasion, for the wonderful bond of love between these two people, for the sincerity of their vows and the strength of their loyalty.

Let us give thanks for the ways in which love comes into our lives, and for all the joys, the possibilities and challenges of marriage and of parenthood.

Let us give thanks for the homes from which .... and .... have come, and for the development of their unique personalities.

Let us wish for .... and .... grace to fulfil the vows and intentions expressed today in lifelong steadfast affection and deepening love.

Option 6:

An Affirmation read by the Guests (printed in the order of service):

.... and ...., we who are your friends are glad to share in your marriage. We offer you our blessings on your life together. We promise you our loving concern in all your joys and sorrows on into the future. Be assured of our ongoing support!

Option 7:

Celebrant:

Loving God, you know our strength, and for our frailty you have compassion.

Be with .... and .... whom you have brought together, in all they undertake.

Grant that we, their friends, along with those who shall be their friends, may sense and understand their needs. Help us to support .... and .... in every way we can, on into the future.

These things we sincerely pray together. Amen.

Item 11: The Dismissal

Option 1:

Celebrant:

.... and .... are given to each other.

We rejoice now in the gift.

May the future fulfil the promise of today; and may the richness of your love grow and be shared for ever.

Go now in peace and love.

Option 2:

Celebrant:

.... and ...., go now in peace, as one.

May your unity last through all your life together, through all the trials and triumphs that lie ahead of you. Go in love: our love goes with you.

Option 3:

Celebrant:

Let us spend a moment in silence thinking of .... and .... as they go forth in their life together.

We extend to you our interest and our good wishes, our friendship and our love in the promises you have made to each other.

May you have long life and every joy together.

Option 4:

Celebrant:

.... and ...., go now in peace and love, and may the Grace of Our Lord Jesus Christ, the Love of God the Father, and the Fellowship of the Holy Spirit be with you both for evermore. Amen.

Option 5:

Celebrant:

Now, may the courage
of the early morning's dawning,
The strength of eternal hills
and wide-open fields,
The joy of silent streams and the gentle wind,
The beauty of flowered gardens and the song of birds,
And the faith of youth be in your hearts:

And the love of God,
That alone can build happiness,
That makes family love flourish
with the radiance of great joy,
be with you always.
And the peace of a quiet evening's ending
and of the midnight,
be yours now and for ever.
Amen.

Item 12: The Blessing

Option 1:

Celebrant:

May the grace of Our Lord Jesus Christ,

The Love of God, and the fellowship of the Holy Spirit be with us all. Amen.

Option 2:

Celebrant:

> May the God and Father of Our Lord Jesus Christ bless, preserve and keep you. May God give you light to guide you, courage to support you, and love to unite you, that you may be faithful to the vows you have made this day, and live together in joy and peace till your life's end. Amen.

Option 3:

Celebrant:

> May God's love refresh the lives of all who have gathered here today. May the vows made by .... and .... remind us of our love for others.
>
> May the friendship we have for them grow in depth and meaning as the years pass. Amen.

Option 4:

Celebrant:

> The Lord bless you and keep you,
> The Lord make his face shine upon you
> and be gracious to you.
> The Lord life up his countenance on you
> and give you peace.

Option 5:

Celebrant:

> The blessing of the God of Sarah and Abraham.
> The blessing of the son, born of the woman Mary,
> the blessing of the Holy Spirit who broods over
> as a mother with her children, by with you all.
> Amen.

Option 6:

The minister / celebrant may lay hands on the heads of the couple. In addition, the assembly may gather around for the laying on of hands:

Pour out your Holy Spirit on .... and .... Continue to give them strength to live together with love and compassion. Fill them with genuine delight in one another. Give them enough creativity to overcome their challenges, and enough humility to forgive their mistakes. Grant them patience and generosity, compassion and tenderness. Bless their home and make it a place of peace and justice. Bring your blessing to their waking and sleeping, to their work and to their play, to their family and to their friends. And, at the last, bring them into your eternal home.

from Long, Kimberly Bracken. Inclusive Marriage Services: A Wedding Sourcebook. Westminster John Knox Press. Kindle Edition.

Option 7:

A Māori language or bicultural ceremony option.

Te Whakapai: Prayer of Blessing.

E Te Matua o tō mātou Ariki a Ihu Karaiti.
Kia tau tō manaaki,
kia ū tonu hoki ki runga i tēnei tāne me tēnei wahine
Manaakitia tō rāua mārena.
Arahina, whangaia, tautokona rāua i roto o tō rāua oranga.
Tukua mai ki a rāua te ora me te rangimārie i ngā wā katoa e ora ai rāua.

Ā, i a rāua e puta atu nei ki te ao, hei tāne pūmau, hei wahine pūmau
Mā te Atua kōrua e manaaki, e tiaki
Māna anō te māramatanga o tōna kanohi e whakawhiti nei ki runga i a kōrua
Mā te Atua kōrua e arataki ki ōna ara
Kia tau ai tōna rangimārie ki runga i a kōrua i ngā rā katoa e ora ai kōrua. Amine.

4 — The reception: recipe for a wedding meal

After the formality of the marriage ceremony, everyone looks forward to the relative informality of the wedding "breakfast." This is the time to relax, to eat, drink and be merry. It's an occasion of happiness, of enjoyment, of celebration, but it also has its own traditional elements; a toast or two, some speeches, the reading of the messages of congratulation and the cutting of the cake. The reception may be fully catered in a restaurant, hotel, or wherever. Or it may be a family effort in a local hall, sports club, or home venue. The style of wedding day you want, and your budget, will dictate the location and style of reception you choose.

Most people enjoy getting a little merry at wedding breakfasts, but make sure you provide non-alcoholic drinks, and plenty of water. If yours is to be a Mormon or a Muslim wedding ceremony, for example, there will of course be no alcohol.

Your reception is a continuation of your marriage celebration. It is not the usual Kiwi style these days to go for long toast lists and lengthy speeches. So, what to do? What are the formalities that do justice to the occasion and enhance the reception without creating that "tolerantly embarrassed" atmosphere that some of us have experienced at wedding receptions? Our suggestion is that you plan what you want according to two principles:

- Keep it simple
- Progress from formality to informality.

Simplicity

In practice, the first principle means keeping the number of speeches to a minimum and telling your speakers that they should be brief and to the point. Unless of course, they are good public speakers and you are confident they will entertain rather than embarrass. A minimum list of formalities might be as follows.

Someone (usually the "toastmaster / toastmistress" or "master / mistress of ceremonies" – the MC) calls for order once the bridal party is seated or otherwise ready. That person then proposes the toast to the bride and groom (or marriage partners), or else calls upon someone else to do so. This normally takes the form of making a short speech to the couple, very often in a humorous style, but also expressing, on behalf of the people who have gathered, good wishes to the couple, and perhaps commenting upon some noteworthy aspect of their lives and relationship. It is very important who you ask to do this task because this toast sets the tone of the formalities at the reception. The toast to the recently married couple expresses what everyone is here for, to wish the couple well and to honour their relationship and intentions.

The groom and/or the bride, or one partner or both partners, then speak in reply to the toast, to convey thanks for help received from parents, bridesmaids, etc., for the gifts received and expressing appreciation for the presence, support and good wishes of family and friends.

The MC then calls upon the best man, and also sometimes the groomsman (if there is one) to read any messages that have been received, from people who are unable to attend. Sometimes it is advisable to appoint someone to censor these messages beforehand. Insensitive or overly profane, obscene, or crude messages can detract from the occasion.

Finally, there is, usually, the cutting of the wedding cake, again introduced by the MC.

This minimum format can be expanded as much as you want. You may wish to consider:

- whether to have a toast to both sets of parents
- whether or not to have a toast to absent friends
- whether and when to have a toast to the bridesmaids

- whether and when to toast any other significant family person or special friend
- whether or not to allow an opportunity for any guest who may wish to make a brief speech to do so.

There are aspects of the wedding reception you may want omit altogether. Many will choose to omit a toast to the bridesmaids. This is viewed by some to be an outmoded and sexist practice. The old custom was for one male to propose the toast and another male to reply on the bridesmaids' behalf. We suggest the bridesmaids be thanked and complimented as part of the groom's reply, and leave it at that. Unless, of course, the bridesmaids (or one of them) want to take the opportunity to say something themselves.

The main thing, however, with regard to these "extra" toasts, is that, if it feels right to you, if it is what you really want and you can get the right people to speak and then propose the appropriate toast, then do it. It's your day, your reception. Celebrate it; acknowledge the significant people in your lives; remember those who can't be with you. Be sincere, authentic and genuine, and include some humour!

Degrees of formality

The second principle – to progress from formality to informality – is a guide to the unfolding of your special day. You will have begun with the most formal element of your special day, the marriage ceremony, even if it is conducted in a relaxed manner and an informal setting.

The next level of formality is the speeches and toasts at the reception; then comes the sharing of a meal together, the relaxing, celebrating merriment of a good wedding reception. We suggest that the best time to have the speech making is before the meal is served.

Your family and friends have gathered, they have shared the formal ceremony with you, they have waited – generally in a convivial atmosphere aided by flowing wine, punch, or whatever – while you have had special photos taken. Now, before they enjoy a delicious meal, let them pause for a moment longer as you capture their attention and thus give them the opportunity of honouring you with their expression of best wishes. They will thank you for it, for they, too, can fully relax once the formalities are over. And if you end these formalities by cutting the cake, what better way to indicate that it is now time to eat and be merry? Before the meal, an appropriate prayer, grace or karakia of thanks for food may be offered.

All this means that the order of events for your overall wedding celebration would be:

- Marriage ceremony
- Wedding photos
- Formal toasts and speeches
- Cutting the cake and reading messages received
- Prayer, Grace, or Karakia (if right for you)
- The reception meal – the "Wedding Breakfast."

Following this format means that all those who are involved in the speech-making can relax after the speeches, along with everyone else, and enjoy the meal. Here, in summary, is a suggested nine-step outline for a wedding reception.

Reception Outline

1. Commencement

The Master or Mistress of Ceremonies (MC) calls for order and the bridal party is seated. The MC calls upon the proposer of the toast to the marriage partners, or the MC proposes the toast.

2. Toast to the marriage partners

The proposer of the toast to the marriage partners makes a short speech, calls upon the guests to "charge your glasses," and proposes the toast. (Note: Allow time for glasses to be filled.)

The MC calls upon one or both marriage partners to reply

3. The marriage partner's speech

A speech of thanks is given by one or both marriage partners, noting the gifts and the contributions of the bridesmaids, family, friends and special helpers.

(Note: traditionally, the groom does not propose any toast, except to the bridesmaids if you wish it.)

4. Reply

The MC calls upon the best man to respond to the marriage partners speech or speeches, and then may read the messages (or the messages may be delayed until after the cake has been cut).

5. The best man's speech

The best man may speak on behalf of bridesmaids/attendants and others who have helped and participated in the ceremony, echoing the appreciation that has been expressed by the marriage partners and perhaps adding a further anecdote or story about the couple.

(Note: Keep it brief, sit down when finished, do not propose any toast.)

6. Other toasts

If there are to be other toasts (for example, to parents, absent friends) or additional speeches (for example, by parents of the bride or groom), they are now introduced by the MC in whatever order has been agreed upon.

7. Cutting of the cake

The MC calls upon the newly-weds to cut the first slice of the wedding cake. The photographer does his/her duty. The cake is removed and cut up for serving later, often with tea or coffee. Alternatively, the cake can be cut at the end of the meal, after dessert has been served.

8. Messages of congratulation

If messages have not already been read at Steps 5 and 6 above, the MC calls upon the best man (and perhaps also the groomsman) to read any messages received.

9. The wedding meal

The MC may call upon the marriage celebrant, or some other appropriate person, to pronounce a karakia or grace – that is, to give thanks for the meal – and thus signal the commencement of the "breakfast." Alternatively, the MC calls upon the father of the bride, or whoever is the "host" of the gathering to either pronounce a grace, offer a simple expression of thanks, or simply issue the invitation to the guests to commence eating.

Advice for all speakers

- Speak clearly, neither too fast nor too slow.
- If you are a confident public speaker and know exactly what you want to say, fine. Otherwise, keep it brief and to the point. Better to say a little well than fluster around making yourself and the listeners embarrassed.
- Be yourself. Be sincere. Say what you feel is right for you regarding the particular speech or toast you have been asked to make.
- Enjoy making your particular contribution to the celebrations.

5 — Celebration and commitment: the honeymoon and beyond

The popular image of the honeymoon is that it is a time of sheer happiness and bliss. Certainly, it's a time for quality time together, following the hustle and bustle of the wedding day. The honeymoon provides an opportunity to relax after a time of considerable stress, irrespective of how the wedding itself went. The importance of the honeymoon is that it marks the first days you have together as a married couple. You are now two individual persons who are committed to one another in the context of a marriage relationship.

Your honeymoon provides you both with an important opportunity to catch your breath before returning to the hurly-burly of everyday existence. It offers the chance to reflect on your relationship. It "cements" and enriches the turning point that was marked publicly by your wedding. It is a time not only for enjoying each other's company in the present, but also for looking ahead, as well as reflecting on where you have come from. You are now married. But just what does it all mean for you?

Over the years we have asked many couples to describe the difference marriage has made, even if they had been living together for some time before their wedding. Generally, couples report a sense of deepened trust in each other's love, having made such a public declaration of their love. Being married, potentially creates a difference in the climate of your commitment, both legally and experientially. You have chosen to identify publicly with the roles and responsibilities, as well as the pleasures and privileges, of partners in marriage. Marriage, ideally, is a commitment to a life-long relationship grounded in love and trust, a commitment to being together through thick and thin, a commitment to grow together in love. Marriage is more than just a private legal contract: it is a relationship recognised by society at large, bringing with it certain traditions and expectations.

Not all of these traditions and expectations are good; neither are they all bad. Each couple has to work out for themselves just what "wife" and "husband," or marriage partner, will mean for their relationship.

For example, do you see your roles as complementary? Do you see them in terms of an equal division of labour, or as expressing a given order of the superiority of the male over the female, or what? There are many views on marriage and many views also on what exactly the roles of husband and wife should be. Yet there is a widespread common understanding which, we suggest, sees the marriage relationship primarily as the coming together of two unique people in a committed, ideally life-long loving partnership. Each of you brings different gifts, abilities and experiences to your marriage. Together you can enrich each other's lives, and the lives of your community. You can complement each other, offering a shared expression of mutual love to the world.

What each partner does is not determined biologically, nor should duties be solely determined by social or religious expectation. What you each do, how you do it and who you become will we suggest, ideally result from a lifetime of intentional mutually agreed decisions. Make time to share about and decide together on issues including your careers and the sharing of domestic duties. Seek always to ensure that your interests, gifts and abilities complement each other to create a beautiful and creative unity. We suggest you schedule in a date together at least monthly to reflect on how you are getting on in your marriage.

Marriage can, we suggest, be defined as a "deep relationship of commitment to togetherness – working and playing lovingly together for the holistic well-being of each partner, and the wider community and world."

Your "togetherness" begins before the wedding day. The marriage ceremony celebrates a relationship that in many respects, of course, has already commenced. Yet it is the moment of stepping into the future in a new context of legal and spiritual commitment. The honeymoon, then, is an important time, for it is the beginning of the future of your marriage. So, plan your time away together well. And don't forget your marriage certificate, especially if you decide to go overseas.

Some of the optional readings for the marriage ceremony talk of marriage as not happening in an instant but as something which is worked at and built up over time. There are many ways in which this growing process can be aided. One of the best is to attend a suitable marriage enrichment course. Find out what's in your area, and treat yourself to time together to experience the challenge and growth of such a course. Usually these are held on week nights, running for several weeks at a time. Sometimes they may be weekend events. However they are run, and whoever they may be run by, they will be, at the very least, a source of stimulation to the growth and development of yourselves as people, and of your relationship. Your marriage celebrant may well be someone who you can continue to meet with from time to time for ongoing encouragement and support.

As well as courses you can attend, there are also a wide range of books on marriage and interpersonal relationships. Many of them have suggested exercises – questions to answer, discussion starters and so on – designed to help you focus on various aspects of your relationship. And if things become really rough, and you feel you need some kind of help, then don't hesitate to consult a counsellor, or your marriage celebrant.

There are many agencies, which can be relied on to provide well-trained people who can help you in confidence. Members of your family, and close friends can be called upon for support, especially those who supported you at your marriage ceremony.

The commitment expressed at your wedding is not to be taken lightly. If your marriage really means something to you, don't be afraid to seek help if or when the going gets tough. Some conflict is inevitable in every relationship.

Although crises in relationships often produce new growth, we do not have to wait for a significant conflict to occur before we grow in our marriage relationship. Indeed, the crises that might precipitate a marriage failure, can be resolved, and lead to renewed depths of love and understanding. The main thing is to be willing always to work at being married, instead of allowing ourselves merely to drift along, assuming all will be well.

It is true that many marriages do, sadly, come unstuck in the end, even though they began with high hopes and the best of intentions. The fact that this might happen should not deter us from a positive approach to setting out on the relationship of marriage. Slowly but surely, creating a healthy and long-lasting marriage is possibly the greatest challenge we will face in life, but it can also be the greatest source of encouragement, reassurance and loving mutual support.

By way of offering some practical guidelines to the development of your marriage relationship beyond the wedding day, we list below some of the qualities that we have found are basic to a healthy relationship. We also offer a set of exercises which you might like to make use of by way of "starters." This will give you some idea of the kind of thing you can find in books that deal more fully with the marriage relationship.

Seven keys to a healthy relationship

Among the many elements that make for a healthy, dynamic relationship, we would list communication, acceptance, sensitivity, understanding, respect, mutual support, and forgiveness as seven of the most important.

Communication

The first key to a healthy relationship is good communication. We are always communicating in our relationships. If I am mad at my partner but say nothing about it, my behaviour and tone of voice in other matters will more than likely communicate that I am uptight. If I don't take time to talk about my anger, then my built-up emotional tension will cause my partner to be edgy, which in turn will send signals back to me, and before we know it "love" seems to be out the door.

Communication is happening all the time, and on many levels.

Words, looks, touches, movement – their presence or absence, their nature and type – are the channels by which we are constantly communicating something of ourselves to our partner.

In a healthy and growing relationship, the agreed goal is always for honest, open and direct communication – ensuring that what we say truly reflects how we feel and that what our partner hears, matches what he or she sees.

And if there is a mismatch – if we say one thing but our partner sees, or feels our true meaning to be something else – then we need to be willing to be challenged, and to respond honestly to our partner's need for clarification. Good communication means making sure we can be understood, and ensuring we are not misunderstood.

Attempts to communicate can all too easily become stalled or blocked due to the barriers we have previously allowed to be built up. For example, pre-judgments which make assumptions about our partner, or place unrealistic demands for certain behaviours on him or her; refusing to really listen to what our partner is trying to say – and finding within ourselves reasons to justify this attitude; engaging in destructive and angry criticism which simply blames the other person, criticising and denigrating our partners thereby undermining the relationship. Sadly, there is a significant amount of family violence in Aotearoa-New Zealand, much of which flows from the inability of couples to communicate honestly and respectfully.

After your marriage you may discover things about your partner which you did not know before, and some of these things may be unsettling. Once you are married, one or both of you may experience physical and/or mental illness. These will test your level of your commitment to your marriage, and to the vows you expressed on the day you married. Good communication and a sincere desire to show love, respect and restraint in all circumstances, can enable resolution of the conflicts which will inevitably arise.

Financial issues are a common source of disagreement and conflict in marriage and other committed relationships. Honest communication in this area is essential. Together, the challenge is to agree on priorities for spending and, wherever possible, saving. Some couples choose to combine all bank accounts and to oversee all spending together. Others choose to trust each other some independence. Where significant financial commitments are made together, for example in taking out a mortgage to purchase a jointly owned home, couples need to be clear on how the mortgage commitments will be met. The same applies to rental payments, and to the purchase of significant items such as cars, appliances etc. and to payments for travel, child-care, donations to charities and gifts. What may appear to be essential expenditure to one partner may not appear so to the other. Sometimes, sacrifices need to be made.

Prejudice can occur simply because we have not checked out with each other how we perceive the roles of "husband" and "wife" operating for us. Ideally this should be discussed during preparation for marriage. Often, couples will find themselves following models inherited from their own parents, which may or may not be helpful. When we talk at, rather than genuinely with, our partner, then we will not be listened to.

Learning to listen is crucial for good communication to take place – listening not only to the words that are being spoken but also to the feelings that lie behind, or are showing through, those words. In other words, listening with both head and heart.

Coming at our partners with statements beginning with "you" is the quickest way to get into a slanging match. For example, "You make me mad," is a form of destructive criticism whereas, "I feel mad," is a simple statement describing the reality of where I am at. This latter statement opens the way to sorting out why I am feeling mad and what we as a couple can do to address and resolve my feelings.

Acceptance

Next to communication, a healthy relationship is built on acceptance. To give our partner the right to be the person he or she is, and not to embark on a subtle process of trying to change them, is to truly accept. Acceptance does not mean blanket approval or the automatic liking of everything about our partner, but without a groundwork of basic acceptance, there is no prospect of mutual growth and change. To insist that our partner conform to our expectations and patterns of behaviour is to do violence to our relationship. It is the opposite of acceptance. We are all unique, individual human beings. Acceptance of the reality of who we are – both ourselves and our partners – will set the scene for growth. If I don't feel accepted, I will be inclined to be defensive and closed. Once I know my partner views me as fundamentally OK, I will be inclined to be open to new possibilities for our relationship, and for development of my own personality within that.

Acceptance is not merely passive. To actively encourage your partner to grow slowly but surely into the kind of person they can become, can be incredibly liberating. Both of you have the opportunity to encourage growth and development in every area of each other's lives; physically, mentally, socially and spiritually.

If each partner in the marriage relationship is encouraged by the other to be and become truly herself or himself, whether it be in the realm of work, or leisure, family life or whatever, then each partner will indeed be blessed. Out of deep love for each other, you have the potential to be able to enhance each other's holistic well-being, throughout your life together.

Sensitivity

As we have mentioned, acceptance doesn't mean that you have to like every little thing about your partner. If there are some things you just can't handle and really struggle with, then that's where honest communication comes in, and, hopefully, the third desirable quality in any relationship comes to the fore: sensitivity. If we value the acceptance we receive from our partner, we need also to be sensitive to their needs and feelings. Acceptance is not a licence to do as we please.

Where something occurs which we find, at least initially, to be unacceptable, then a resolution may potentially be found through sensitive communication. Submission to and forced acceptance of something we genuinely find to be unacceptable for the sake of "love" will, in the end, undermine and destroy that love.

There is a story of a man who, on the first morning after the wedding, began to suck fried egg through a piece of fried bread. His partner nearly fainted with horror. Good communication demands that each couple talk about such practices – and more serious ones – openly.

Acceptance means allowing each partner the freedom to be themselves; sensitivity means being aware of each other's feelings and concerned enough not to want deliberately to upset or antagonise each other. In the example quoted, the end result might be that the man chooses to change a breakfast habit. Or that he agrees to eat this way only when his partner is not around. Or perhaps his partner might decide after talking and thinking about it, that eating eggs in this way is acceptable behaviour after-all!

Understanding

Understanding ourselves and our partners is a lifelong adventure in communication. We all have our dreams and desires, our fears and anxieties, strengths and weaknesses – the quirks and peculiarities that make us uniquely who we are. These form the raw material not only of our personality but also of the relationship which involves the union of two personalities. We listen to each other because we want to understand each other. We know we are truly loved when we know we are understood and accepted for who and what we are.

The maturing of love beyond the mystique of chemistry and mutual desire of physical attraction is directly related to the cultivation of mutual understanding in a climate of sensitive communication and acceptance of each other. For people of Christian or other theistic faith, such mutual understanding can be progressively deepened through praying together, in the context of a shared awareness of God's loving and understanding presence.

Respect

In a healthy and growing marriage relationship, respect for each other as individual persons, building on basic acceptance, is vitally important. Each partner has their own unique personality, capabilities, aspirations, hopes, desires and dreams. In the context of a loving relationship these need to be accepted for what they are, and each person should be respected by the other. Respect means honouring each other as persons of value and worth. It undergirds many of the qualities we have touched on.

Furthermore, as the initial "romantic" love fades with time, dishes, nappies, overtime, tiredness, mortgage repayments and whatever, mature love evolves, based on the foundation of mutual respect.

Together with understanding, respect is the basis of that kind of deep friendship which is the mark of a healthy marriage relationship. To be not only lovers, but to be true friends, is born out of a climate of mutual respect. This is indeed precious and worth more than gold.

Mutual Support

Closely allied to respect is the quality of support that each offers to the other in the partnership of life. This is where respect is expressed in action. Once decisions have been agreed upon in regard to activities and obligations that each may undertake as an individual, e.g. career, finances, leisure, voluntary association, then it is vital to the health of the relationship that each partner feels the genuine support of the other in the enactment of those decisions. The demands of careers may clash. The needs of family may conflict with commitments to a sports team. Time out as individuals may compete with time together as a couple or family. Whatever the practical circumstance, the measure of successfully coping, adjusting, and striking a satisfactory balance will reflect the degree to which the relationship displays genuine mutual support. One-way support is inadequate: that is likely to leave one partner feeling that they are doing all the compromising and adjusting. Mutual support requires two-way give-and-take in a climate of co-equal valuing of what it is that each other seeks to do and achieve.

Forgiveness

This final "key" is not simply a religious word or idea – it is one of the most powerful dynamics in a robust relationship. Along with the ability to own up to mistakes – to say we are sorry to each other because we truly respect each other as persons – the capacity actually to forgive one another is vital in clearing the way for new growth and the deepening of love. Indeed, it is the necessary counterpart to acceptance, and to be effective it requires open and honest communication. It is the fruit of sensitivity and an expression of understanding. It allows for a profound acceptance of each other as persons, yet it does not hide from the pain or provocation that gave rise to the need for forgiveness in the first place. Forgiveness is a two-way street. It requires that the partner who is the source of the pain, provocation, or whatever, is able to acknowledge this and accept the consequent negative consequences for their partner as valid. The offending partner needs to be willing to sincerely apologise, and make amends wherever possible, before they can legitimately receive the forgiveness that the aggrieved partner will hopefully be able to offer.

To demand forgiveness from our partner, as if it were a conjugal right is not respectful, and may well destroy a relationship. True sincerely granted forgiveness however, is the oil that keeps the engine of love running smoothly. Forgiveness sets us free to begin again, to learn from our mistakes, and to do our very best not to make them again. If we truly love our partner, we will be honest with them about our desire to live out our marriage vows. There is an opportunity for growth in every crisis, and forgiveness is often the key to enabling each partner to make a fresh start.

We consider these seven components to be major dynamics in any healthy marriage relationship. More could be said about them, and more could be added. You may well be able to think of others. We suggest that you sit down and share with each other how you feel about the experience of these seven dynamics in your life together. After sharing in this way, discuss what other relationship dynamics are important to you, and why.

Some relationship-building exercises

Share with each other

What was the personal quality that most attracted you to your partner when you were first together? Look at your relationship now. What is it in your partner's behaviour that is now deepening this attractiveness? What is undermining it?

An exercise in touch

Each take turn in laying your head in your partner's lap. Both close your eyes. The partner in whose lap the other's head is resting traces, feels and caresses the other's face using the fingertips. Do this for about three minutes, then tell each other what it was like, and what you learned both from touching and being touched.

Learning to express feelings and reactions

Take turns in asking each other the following questions and sharing your feelings and reactions to each other's answers.

> Right now, I am feeling …
>
> I usually handle frustrations by …
>
> When I feel rejected, I …
>
> When I feel your full acceptance of me, I …
>
> I need your support most when I …
>
> When I don't like myself, I feel …
>
> What turns me off most is …
>
> I feel very affectionate when …
>
> For me, a sense of belonging to each other means …
>
> I feel happiest when …

The above are examples of the kinds of exercises you will find in many modern books of marriage and interpersonal relationships. If you liked doing them, and found them helpful, then you are ready to look for similar resources. Perhaps also, as we indicated at the beginning of this chapter, you could consider a couples' course if you have not already experienced one. May the commitment to marriage you made and celebrated on your wedding day, find fulfilment and growth: it can only do so if you are prepared to actively work on your marriage.

Sometimes, after every effort has been made to restore a broken relationship the best decision all things considered, is to end the marriage and apply for a dissolution (divorce). The Uniting Church of Australia has prepared a pastoral service of healing for those whose marriage has ended, or is ending, which we would commend. See: https://assembly.uca.org.au/marriage-services

Our hope for you is that this is not something you will have to face. Rather, it is our hope that the record of your wedding day will contain many happy anniversaries added to it for many years to come.

Part Two – Marriage Records

1 — Planning your wedding: a practical guide

To assist the planning of your wedding the following arrangements checklist, ceremony selection list, and reception summary and checklist have been prepared. By keeping track of decisions made, and progress on arrangements that are underway, you can help lessen the stress that people often experience, especially if you are not used to organising such complex events. It can also be useful to keep such records in one handy place. Once you have read through the chapters on practical preliminaries and the structure and plan of the wedding ceremony you will be ready to tackle the decisions that these lists call for.

Preparation checklist

☐ Our marriage celebrant ....

Marriage licence:
  ☐ Applied for ....
  ☐ Collected/received ....

Place of wedding:
  ☐ Reservation/booking confirmed ....
  ☐ Date and time ....

Bridal party confirmed:
  ☐ Chief bridesmaid or Matron of honour ....
  ☐ Best man ....
  ☐ Other attendants ....

Flowers:
  ☐ Venue ....

- ☐ Bridal party ....
- ☐ Other ....

Other Arrangements:
- ☐ Organist/other music ....
- ☐ Ushers confirmed ....
- ☐ Photographer arranged/confirmed ....
- ☐ Car(s) arranged/booked ....
- ☐ Guest list completed ....

Invitations:
- ☐ Emailed ....
- ☐ Printed ....
- ☐ Sent ....
- ☐ "Wish list" of wedding gifts compiled ....

Bridal apparel:
- ☐ Wedding dress ....
- ☐ Bridesmaid(s) dress(es) ....

Suit hire/purchase:
- ☐ Bridegroom ....
- ☐ Best man/groomsmen ....

Gifts for attendants:
- ☐ Decided ....
- ☐ Obtained ....

Wedding ring(s):
- ☐ Selected ....
- ☐ Collected ....
- ☐ Other arrangements ....

Marriage ceremony selection list

As you go through the options for your ceremony, note your initial preferences. You may find you change your mind. Final decisions need to be made in consultation with your celebrant.

Our options:

Section I

    1. Introduction ....

    2. Prayer ....

    3. Optional reading ....

Section II

    4. Declaration of intention ....

    5. The giving and affirmation ....

    6. The vows ....

    7. The exchange of rings ....

    8. The pronouncement ....

Section III

    9. Reading on love ....

    10. Conclusion ....

    11. The dismissal ....

    12. The blessing ....

Together with:

    13. The signing of the register – placed after? ....

    14. Song/hymn/music choice ....

    Placed after? ....

    Placed after? ....

The reception: a summary

Style of wedding reception meal

What kind of occasion to you want? A formal setting? Buffet style?

Named place cards for the guests? Many options are possible. You can be guided by your caterer, if you are to have one, and/or the host of your reception. In the end, what you do will depend on how formal or informal you want your day to be. Think about our suggestion that all formalities, including cutting the cake and the reading of messages, take place before the meal is served. That way everyone can relax and enjoy the meal. It also means the cake can be cut and ready for serving with tea or coffee as soon as the breakfast meal is finished.

Toasts and speeches

Do you want the full range of toasts and speeches or just a few? Which ones will you have? Who are you going to ask to do them? If you want to keep it really simple, all that is required is a toast to the wedding partners. One partner, traditionally the groom, gives a speech which is largely one of thanks.

Cutting the cake

The cake may be cut immediately following the speeches or, if left until the end of the meal, after dessert is served. Remember, though, to allow time for it to be cut up so it can be served with tea or coffee not too long after people have finished desert.

Reading of messages

Messages of congratulations and best wishes received from people who are not present at the reception are normally read out by the best man, together with the groomsman (and/or the bridesmaids too, if you want) at some appropriate point, usually after the cutting of the cake. Often this is the last item of formality.

Social time and/or dance option

Very often people find that they are limited in the number of guests they are able to formally invite to the wedding and reception. Sometimes friends and acquaintances whom you have not been able to include at your wedding reception might choose attend the wedding ceremony. This works well enough when the ceremony is at one location and the reception is somewhere else. It's a bit more difficult if they are both more or less at the same place.

One way around this, especially if you plan a late afternoon wedding and your reception venue is suitable, is to have a social time and/or dance to follow your wedding reception. That way you can increase the number of people you can invite to join with you in celebrating your marriage. This will require additional arrangements, including arranging the recorded music or live band, and deciding whether or not to provide supper.

Reception checklist

Reception:
- ☐ Venue booked ....
- ☐ Catering confirmed ....
- ☐ Flowers/decor arranged ....
- ☐ Music ....
- ☐ Other ....
- ☐ Master of Ceremonies ....

Proposer(s) of toast(s):
- ☐ Toast list finalised ....
- ☐ Proposers confirmed ....

Other speakers:
- ☐ Replying to toasts ....
- ☐ Other speeches ....

Wedding Cake:
- ☐ Arranged/ordered ....
- ☐ When cut and served ....

Social/dance following reception:
- ☐ Music ....
- ☐ Supper ....

2 — Keeping Account: A wedding and anniversary record

Our Wedding Day

Our marriage celebrant: ....

Venue: ....

Date and time: ....

Our witnesses: ....

Chief bridesmaid: ....

Best man: ....

Others in our bridal party (as applicable):

Bridesmaids: ....

Groomsmen: ....

Flower girls: ....

Page boys: ....

Gifts received:

> We suggest that you keep a detailed record of the wedding gifts you receive, and who has given you each gift. It is advisable to ask one or more members of your wedding party to compile this list for you. A month or two after your ceremony you can then send thank you notes.

Our anniversaries

Number	Name	How celebrated
First	Cotton	
Second	Paper	
Third	Leather	
Fourth	Fruit or flowers	
Fifth	Wooden	
Sixth	Sugar or candy	
Seventh	Woollen or copper	
Eighth	Bronze or pottery	
Ninth	Willow pattern or pottery	
Tenth	Tin	
Eleventh	Steel	
Twelfth	Silk and fine linen	
Thirteenth	Lace	
Fourteenth	Ivory	
Fifteenth	Crystal	
Twentieth	China	
Twenty-fifth	Silver	
Thirtieth	Pearl	
Thirty-fifth	Coral	
Fortieth	Ruby	
Forty-fifth	Sapphire	
Fiftieth	Golden	
Fifty-fifth	Emerald	
Sixtieth	Diamond	

Part Three – Having Children

Part Three – Having Children

1 — Welcoming children

Many marriages result in, or sometimes follow, the birth of children. For all the demands they might make, children most typically are greeted as a blessing. They bring joy and delight, as well as sleepless nights and not a little anxiety!

In welcoming a new life, most, if not all, cultures have some ceremony at which the new-born child is incorporated into the family and community, and where the child may be formally named and "blessed." Although contemporary understandings of family vary considerably, many people still associate commitment to marriage with a commitment to nurturing new life in a family. Ideally, all children will be embraced by their parent's sincere intention to create a secure and loving home and family environment for them.

Whatever the nature of the relationship of the parents, it is often the case that, where there is a commitment to a stable and shared life together, there is also a desire to celebrate the event of a new life brought to birth. Traditionally such celebrations, in a formal context, have been associated with Christian religious acts such as baptism or "christening."

Religious communities all have their different formal customs for recognising birth and incorporating the new life into the community. In the context of the Christian heritage of New Zealand the most common practice has been baptism. Ever since the beginning of Christianity, baptism, in both its adult and infant variants, has been the formal rite of entry into the Christian Church.

One traditional belief was that infant baptism actually made the individual a "Christian." This explains the origin of the English verb "to christen." A baby that was christened was, and still is in some churches, regarded as having been made a Christian by that act.

Typically, however, for most churches a baby who is baptised will have the opportunity later as a teenager or adult to confirm their baptism, should they wish to, so making a mature decision to identify as a Christian. Traditionally, infant baptism is the time when babies are given their "Christian" name. However, the naming of children (an important component of family identity) can be incorporated into other more secular ceremonies. The names which we give our children are very significant, and a blessing or ceremony of welcome for a child can provide the context for celebrating the bestowing of a unique and special name, for each unique and precious child.

There are a number of rites or liturgies available for giving thanks for the birth of a child, or the blessing of a child, in a Christian context. For example, see the document *Thanksgiving for the birth of a Child* on the Methodist Church of Aotearoa-New Zealand's website:

http://www.methodist.org.nz/faith_and_order

Increasingly, many are recognising the significant difference between an act of thanksgiving and infant baptism. A thanksgiving ceremony can be an occasion of family celebration without the need to own any particular religious identity or beliefs. However, the rite of infant baptism (also a celebration) requires a specific relationship to, and understanding of, the Christian faith. Infant baptism (even where it is called "christening") requires the parents to make certain promises on behalf of their child and in respect of their ongoing relationship to the Christian Church. These are serious matters, not to be taken lightly. So, what do you do if that is not for you, yet you want some dignified, even spiritual, act of recognition of and thanksgiving for this new life? Some people may simply have a social gathering of family and close friends to celebrate the arrival of a new baby. That may suffice. But what if you want something more – yet not a baptism or christening?

The answer that many parents have found is to have a short celebratory ceremony of thanksgiving and blessing. This can be conducted by a minister, priest or pastor – or a celebrant or friend who has some skill in these kinds of events. Such a ceremony need not take place in a Church. It may be an informal gathering in a family home, or any other suitable location.

Such a ceremony can be reflective and very meaningful. It may have a religious or spiritual element. But it need not address or include issues such as commitment of the child to a particular religion. It can leave to one side the question of the parents' specific relationship to a church, or indeed to any faith community, which is otherwise a prerequisite to the enactment of a church rite. It can focus primarily on the fact that the new-born child is dearly loved by his or her family, and provide an opportunity to celebrate and express this love.

New Zealand celebrant, Rochelle Fleming, has put it rather well:

> When a baby is born, along come all the sleepless nights and there is little time to stop, reflect, thank and celebrate, all of which you can do with a welcoming or naming ceremony. Traditionally, such ceremonies take place within the first year. However, some parents choose to incorporate a ceremony with the first birthday of their child. There are no firm rules. You might decide to have a naming day for all your children, or all the grandchildren recognising the completion of your family or the family at large.
>
> If you want to you can include some religious content such as a prayer or blessing. Older siblings can participate in various ways, the parents might choose friends or family members to be mentors / guardians / guide parents / godparents/ fairy godmothers to the baby. Music and poetry or stories can be included as well.
>
> *From Rochelle Fleming's website.*
> *See Appendix 3 References.*

The following formats provide a structure and plan, and also a few options, upon which parents, perhaps together with other close family, friends, or minister/celebrant, can construct a suitable ceremony. Although the content of the first two options reflect a Christian religious context, an alternative spiritual, or a purely secular, ceremony could be constructed if you wish, simply by using the basic format but substituting material of your own choosing. As with a wedding ceremony, it is appropriate and customary to have a time of fellowship and sharing together over food and drink, following any blessing of a child ceremony. And remember, all these ceremonies can be held in a Church, a home, or other suitable venue, including outdoor venues. Friends and family can be included as readers and musicians.

2 — Celebrating birth: ceremony formats

Ceremony 1

The format for this ceremony might include any or all elements of the following:

- Words of introduction
- A reflective reading or meditation
- An act of promise by the parents
- An act of promise by the godparents
- An affirmation by family and friends
- An act of blessing
- Prayer of thanksgiving
- Lord's Prayer, or other 'general prayer' or further reflective reading
- Words of conclusion/Benediction

As with the multi-choice marriage ceremony, there is always the additional option of writing, editing, compiling, omitting, expanding, or otherwise modifying, including coming up with other material of your own.

Format options:

This ceremony can be constructed from the following options. Use the options provided as a starting point and follow the same principle that governs the marriage ceremony. It is your ceremony, so let it reflect who and where you are, and have fun preparing it! Once you have put it together, all you need is to gather your family and friends around you and have your chosen celebrant conduct the ceremony for you. On the day, you may like to precede your special ceremony by welcoming everyone and explaining what is going to happen, and why.

Introduction

Option 1

Celebrant:

This is a ceremony in which we gather together to express our love and thanks for the gift of ...., daughter/son of .... and............ .

We gather to pray God's blessing upon her/him, and hope that she/he will grow into faith and respond to her/his calling.

We acknowledge the warmth and love of her family, and we pray .... will come to know the many wondrous ways of faith and life.

So, let us celebrate the miracle of life, and recognise the goodness of God.

Life is a gift
It is not earned
It is not bought
It is not made
It is given to us
It is a gift from God.

Option 2:

Celebrant:

.... and .... would like to welcome family and friends to this special occasion in which we celebrate the miracle of life.

Life is a gift
It is not earned
It is not bought
It is not made
It is given to us
It is a gift from God.

So, we have all come together today to give thanks for the precious gift that is .... We pray God's blessing upon him/her and all he/she becomes.

Option 3:

Celebrant:

> .... and .... would like to welcome family and friends to this special occasion. We gather together today to celebrate the miracle of .... and ....'s precious son/daughter's (............'s) birth
>
> .... was born on ....
>
> .... and ....'s lives have been enriched and truly blessed by their son/daughter's ....'s arrival. They are truly grateful for this precious new life. In spite of the broken nights and all the challenges of parenthood, ... and .... deeply love .... They are deeply committed to raising their daughter/son, in an environment of love, safety and devoted care.

A reflective reading or mediation

Option 1: Jesus blesses little children

Celebrant:

> Some people brought children to Jesus for him to place his hands on them, but the disciples scolded the people. When Jesus noticed this, he was angry and said to his disciples, "Let the children come to me, and do not stop them, because the Kingdom of God belongs to such as these. I assure you that whoever does not receive the Kingdom of God like a child will never enter it." Then he took the children in his arms, placed his hands on each of them, and blessed them.
>
> Mark 10:13–16

Option 2: A meditation on Psalm 8

Celebrant:

> O God,
> How full of wonder and splendour you are!
> I see the reflections of your beauty and hear the sounds of your majesty wherever I turn.
>
> Even the babbling of babes and the laughter of children spell out Your name in indefinable syllables.
>
> When I gaze into star-studded skies and attempt to comprehend the vast distances, I contemplate in utter amazement my Creator's concern for me.
>
> I am dumbfounded that you should care personally about me.
>
> And yet you have made me in your image,
> You have called me Your child.
>
> O God, how full of wonder and splendour you are!
>
> Paraphrase by Leslie Brandt

Option 3: "Children learn what they live"

Celebrant [or another person to read this]:

> If children live with criticism – they learn to condemn.
>
> If children live with hostility – they learn to fight.
>
> If children live with ridicule – they learn to be shy.
>
> If children live with shame – they learn to feel guilty.
>
> If children live with tolerance – they learn to be patient.
>
> If children live with encouragement – they learn confidence.
>
> If children live with praise – they learn to appreciate.
>
> If children live with fairness – they learn justice.
>
> If children live with security – they learn to have faith.

If children live with approval – they learn to like themselves.

If children live with acceptance and friendship – they learn to find love.

Unknown

Option 4: "Speak to us of children"

Celebrant [or another person to read this]:

Your children are not your children –
They are the sons and daughters
of life's longing for itself.

They come through you but not from you:
And though they are with you
yet they belong not to you.

You may give them your love but not your thoughts –
for they have their own thoughts.

You may house their bodies, but not their souls –
for their souls dwell in the house of tomorrow,
which you cannot visit, not even in your dreams.

You may strive to be like them,
but seek not to make them like you:

For life goes not backward nor tarries with yesterday.

You are the bows from which your children as living arrows are sent forth.

Kahlil Gibran, The Prophet

An act of promise by the parents

Option 1:

Celebrant:

It is fitting today that we should ask the parents to make appropriate promises with respect to their relationship with their child.

To the parents:

.... and ...., do you promise, as far as you are able, to build your family life on love and truth, on tolerance and encouragement, on fairness and security?

Parents: Yes, we do.

Celebrant:

And do you also promise to do your best to encourage .... to become herself/himself, to value human relationships and appreciate the gift of life, to strive for the best in whatever she/he chooses to do?

Parents: Yes, we do.

Option 2:

Celebrant:

It is fitting today that we should ask the parents to make appropriate promises with respect to their relationship with their child(ren).

(To the parents) .... and ...., do you promise, as far as you are able, to build your family life on love and truth, on tolerance and encouragement, on fairness and security?

Parents: Yes, we do.

Celebrant:

Will you also promise to encourage .... to discover and develop her abilities and talents whilst allowing him/her to choose his/her own path in life? Will you strive to teach him/her care and respect for all people?

Parents: Yes, we will.

Option 3:

Celebrant:

It is fitting that, as an expression and focus of our thanksgiving, we should ask the parents to make appropriate promises with respect to their relationship with their child(ren).

(To the parents): .... and ...., do you promise, as far as you are able, to build your family life on love and respect, trust, tolerance and forgiveness?

Parents: Yes, we do.

Celebrant:

And do you also promise to do your best to encourage .... to achieve the full potential of which she/he is capable, to value human relationships and appreciate the gift of life with all its happiness and pain?

Parents: Yes, we do.

An act of promise by the Godparents

Celebrant:

[Names of parents] have asked [Name of godparent(s)] to act as godparent(s) to their child/children ....

Do you, as ....'s godparent(s), pledge your support of .... in their role as parents; and do you promise, so far as you are able, to stand by .... throughout (his/her/their) growth to full maturity?

Response: I/We do.

An affirmation by family and friends

Celebrant:

And will you, ... and ....'s families and friends, do all you are able to support and encourage .... and .... as they seek to nurture and care for ....

Response: We will.

An act of blessing

Celebrant (takes child and says):

> ...., The Lord bless you and watch over you;
> The Lord make his face to shine upon you
> and be gracious to you;
> The Lord look kindly on you and give you peace.
>
> Amen

(Celebrant returns child to a parent)

Prayer of thanksgiving

Celebrant:

> For the gift of life;
> For the glory and wonder of the world
> For the worldwide human family.
> Born to give and born to receive,
> Born to help and born to be helped,
> Born to lead and born to be led,
> Born to love and born to be loved.
> Response by family and friends:
> O God of Life and Love,
> We give our thanks.

> For the trials which children bring us;
> For the pains of growing, the hurts of learning;
> For the joys which children bring us;
> For their laughter and innocence,
> their love and unquestioning trust;
> For ...., and for the love of her/his parents:

Optional response by family and friends:

> O God of Life and Love,
> We give our thanks.
> Amen.

The Lord's Prayer (*may be spoken together*)

> Our Father in heaven,
> hallowed be your name,
> your kingdom come,
> your will be done,
> on earth as in heaven.
> Give us today our daily bread.
> Forgive us our sins
> as we forgive those who sin against us.
> Save us from the time of trial
> and deliver us from evil.
> For the kingdom, the power, and the glory are yours
> now and for ever.
> Amen.

The Benediction

May be said by Celebrant, or sung by everyone to the tune Edelweiss:

> May the Lord, gracious God,
> Love and keep you forever.
> May God's power and God's grace
> Bless our every endeavour.
> Lift up your eyes and seek God's face
> And God's grace forever.
> May the Lord, gracious God
> Love and keep you forever.

Ceremony 2

This is a form of ceremony potentially suited to a solo parent who wishes to provide a meaningful celebration for their child, as well as to any couple likewise celebrating the birth of their child. It may have a religious or spiritual flavour, or not, as suited to the context.

Format options:

- The Celebrant offers a warm welcome to family and friends
- A suitable favourite song or hymn may be sung
- A suitable reading or reflection
- The parent/s come forward with their child and, if they wish, with any other children they may already have. They are given the opportunity to share their personal experiences of welcoming their new child into their family, and the opportunity to express their deep love for their child (or children).

    The celebrant then invites the parent/s to make promises to their new child. The following options can be shared alternatively by the parents, or one parent can speak on behalf of both parents, or when only one parent is present, the words can be modified accordingly.

Options for a promise by the parent(s) (*any one or more may be used*)**:**

Parent/s:

> ...., today I/we stand here as your parent/s. I/We prayed for you and loved you when you were just a thought in my/our mind/s and I/we have prayed over you and loved you since you came into existence.

Parent/s:

> Today, ..., I/we promise to love you forever. We promise that we will teach you the truth, and to renounce evil and injustice. We promise to surround you with goodness and mercy so that you may grow to value life in all of life's beautiful fullness.

Parent/s:

We promise to teach you the foundations of the Christian faith: the love and majesty of God, the life, death and resurrection of Jesus Christ, and the comfort and guidance of the Holy Spirit.

Parent/s:

We promise to teach you to love the people who share this world with you, and to work alongside us for the good of all people.

Parent/s:

We will do all these things, not in our own strength, but with the help of God and of others.

- If there are Godparent/s, they may make promises to the parents to support them in bringing up their child in the knowledge and love of God, and to support them in fulfilling the promises they have made to their child.
- A second suitable reflective reading
- A blessing prayer [*a Christian example is given; there are many other options*]

Celebrant:

............, may God bless you this day and always. May God watch over you and protect you throughout your life. May you grow up surrounded by the love of God. May God's love flow into your life through the love of your family and the care of your friends. As you grow may you experience more and more the truth that God loves you.

May you grow one day to the point of accepting the friendship of Jesus Christ, and discover what it means to live your life in the power and joy of the Holy Spirit.

.... I sign you with the sign of the cross in the name of God our Creator, Redeemer and Sustainer. May you grow in love and grace, knowing that you are a dearly loved child of God, and may you come to know that you are dearly loved by your parents, by your family and by us all. May you forever continue to be bound to God and may your parents' love be deepened through their shared love for you. May God bless you now and always. These things we pray in the name of Jesus Christ, the children's saviour. Amen.

- The presentation of a candle.
- A closing favourite song or hymn.
- Closing words (may include a benediction).

Ceremony 3

A secular (non-religious) welcoming and naming ceremony. This is highly flexible and open to incorporating many fun elements and activities. After all, this is a joyful occasion.

Format options:

Here are a few ideas as provided by Rochelle Fleming via her website:

https://www.nzweddingcelebrant.co.nz/single-post/2016/06/15/Welcome-baby-%E2%80%93-naming-ceremonies

- Goodwill wishes are read out by friends and family at the ceremony, or tied to a tree or placed into a time capsule or book.
- A tree is planted to represent growth and change
- Butterflies are released to represent new beginnings
- Hand-printed ceramic tiles or a family fingerprint tree are created and kept to help remember the occasion

You may well think of other ideas. And remember that all these sorts of creative activities can be accompanied by readings, reflections, poetry, and music. Feel free to draw on any of the options and words from Ceremonies 1 and 2 – or simply write or find your own!

Part Four – Same-Sex ceremonies

Getting Married in New Zealand – Te Mārenatanga ki Aotearoa

1 — A new development

Marriage practices – and various understandings of marriage – do not stand alone. They are in constant dialogue with, and are influenced by, the cultures in which they are embedded. The advent of formalised same-sex relationships by way of civil union, wedding and blessing ceremonies represents one of the most far-reaching social developments in recent times. For some it is still controversial; for others it may be something that seems new and different. Many people today believe that this new practice has evolved to bring justice and fairness to marriage relationships, regardless of each partner's gender identity. The new law in Aotearoa-New Zealand affirms everyone's right to their own identity, with love and commitment the key elements, regardless of sexual orientation.

Members and adherents of the many and varied Christian faith communities in our land continue to differ considerably in their attitudes towards same-sex marriage. For example, in Aotearoa-New Zealand, most Christian Church authorities do not offer same-sex marriage. However, while the Anglican Church in Aotearoa, New Zealand and Polynesia does not permit its priests to conduct same-sex marriages, it has recently (in 2018) agreed to the blessing of same-sex marriages (following a civil marriage) by a priest who has been authorised by his/her bishop. Ordained clergy of The Methodist Church of New Zealand, and also the Uniting Church of Australia, are permitted (but not required) to conduct same-sex marriages in their Church buildings and elsewhere. The Methodist Church Conference in 1993 decided to order its life in accordance with NZ Human Rights Act (1991), an Act which very clearly prohibits any discrimination on the grounds of sexual orientation. The policy of the Methodist Church on same-sex marriage (and on acceptance of gay and lesbian members and clergy) is seen to be consistent with human rights as enshrined in New Zealand legislation.

The Metropolitan Church in New Zealand offers same-sex marriage ceremonies. The Metropolitan Church was founded in Los Angeles in 1968 in response to oppression against minorities, particularly the gay community. The Uniting Church of Australia became the first Australian denominational Church to endorse same-sex marriage in September 2018, and thus the first in Australia to offer gay and lesbian Christians the option of a church ceremony. This move came nine months after same-sex marriage was made legal in Australia. Australia's Uniting Church now stands with Canada's United Church of Christ, the United States' Episcopal Church (ECUSA), the Presbyterian Church in the United States (PCUSA), the Scottish Episcopal Church, the Lutheran Church of Sweden, together with the Methodist Church in Aotearoa-New Zealand in being open to marrying same-sex couples. Quakers (The Society of Friends) in New Zealand also permit same-sex marriage.

The traditional Christian understanding of marriage, upheld still by most Christian Churches is that marriage is defined as being exclusively between a man and a woman. The Bible can, of course, be used to defend this, just as the Bible can be used to prohibit the ordination of women, and the sanctioning of slavery and apartheid. The "deep justice" themes present in the Bible can, we suggest, be used in support of a redefinition of Christian marriage to embrace partners of the same sex.

In support of this, Marvin M. Ellison (2004) adopts a "justice lens." He presents a passionate experience-informed and thorough academically researched biblical, justice and human-rights-based theological justification for same-sex marriage. Daniel C. Maguire, Professor of Moral Theology at Marquette University, having analysed Ellison's book, writes, "Heterosexuals have no monopoly on love. Marvin Ellison brilliantly shows in this book that the right to marry is a human right, not an award for being heterosexual."

A relatively recent new book, *Changing our mind* (2014) by the American evangelical ethicist, David Gushee, has helped many people to re-examine their understanding of homosexuality. Once an attitudinal change has been initiated in the direction of inclusive love, some who were formerly opposed to homosexuality on theological grounds, can and indeed do change their minds and come to an acceptance of same-sex marriage. Such a change of mind may take several years, however. And it is not encouraged by many Christian Churches, still, as they regard such a change as counter to their understanding and interpretation of scriptural teaching. Other religions, including traditional forms of Islam and orthodox Judaism, to name but two, continue to forbid same-sex relationships and hold fast to their traditional understanding of marriage. Traditional Islam continues to allow for polygamy, with one man able to have up to four wives. Not all law systems of Muslim majority countries endorse this, however. New Zealand law does not permit polygamy.

In 2012, when the New Zealand Parliament was discussing the first reading of the Marriage (Definition of marriage) Amendment Bill, the Rev Dr David Clark, a Presbyterian Minister and Labour MP for North Dunedin, explained why he would vote in favour of the new legislation, in these words:

> The strongest support for marriage equality that I have experienced has come from the age group most likely to be engaging in marriage in the future. It is for those people who will be inheriting and carrying forward the institution of marriage that I am supporting the bill. I am mindful that many of my colleagues from across the House who would claim a strong faith background do not support this view. I am respectful of their beliefs, and although I know that they have carefully and prayerfully examined their own consciences, I am mindful that they may come to a different view from mine. My thoughts are with them and with people wrestling personally with the impact of this bill on their lives.
>
> *Hansard Debates:*
> *Marriage [Definition of Marriage] Amendment Bill*
> *– First Reading, 29 August 2012.*

As mentioned in our preface, committed homosexual and LGBTI marriages are legal and celebrated today in Aotearoa-New Zealand. To be a civil (secular) marriage celebrant in NZ today, requires a willingness to officiate at all marriages, including ceremonies between partners of the same sex.

2 — Marriage ceremony resources and options

Kimberly Bracken Long and David Maxwell (2015) provide four helpful inclusive marriage liturgies. The first is for general use, or for couples who are marrying for the first time. The second is for couples who have been in a long-term committed relationship. The third is for couples who have children living at home and are blending families. The fourth is for couples in which one partner is not Christian (useful for interfaith couples and those who have little or no connection to the Church). If you can access this book (see Appendix 3: Reference list, at the end of this book) you may find it very helpful.

Other suitable ceremony options are provided in Church sources from around the world. For example:

- An order for marriage from the second edition of the United Church of Christ (USA) *Book of Worship*
- An adaptation of a wedding service from *Celebrate God's Presence*, the worship book of the United Church of Canada
- An adaptation of a gender-neutral "sacred union" service (not a marriage service) provided by the Uniting Network Australia, a national network of lesbian, gay, bisexual, transgender and intersex people working for safety and equality in the Uniting Church in Australia
- An adaptation of the First Order of Marriage found in the *Book of Common Order*, the worship book of the Church of Scotland
- An adaptation of Rite 1 in the *Book of Common Worship*, the worship book of the Presbyterian Church, USA.

All of the above provide an excellent range of wording options for same-sex marriage services, complementing the modified formats that have rendered most of our own options gender inclusive.

The wording used in same-sex marriage services (or in the blessing of same-sex relationships) can be prepared so as to be appropriate for each couple.

For example, from an Episcopal Church (USA) service resource:

Celebrant (addressed to each of the couple in turn):

Do you take this man/woman/person to be your lawfully wedded husband/wife/spouse?

Or:

............, do you freely and unreservedly offer yourself to ....?

Response: I do.

Celebrant:

Will you live together in faithfulness and holiness of life as long as you both shall live?

Response: I will.

The appropriate wording for the full ceremony would be agreed upon before the service, and practiced carefully, as with all the other ceremonies we provide in this book.

Similarly, vows can be prepared to give expression to the depth of love present between same-sex couples, using language which is appropriate and meaningful for each couple.

For example, here is a "partnership vow" from a Uniting Network (Australia) ceremony:

Celebrant:

Two partners, in giving themselves to each other in love, reflect the love of Christ for his Church. The companionship and comfort of marriage enables the full expression of physical love between the two partners.

............, will you give yourself to .... to be her/his partner, to live together in the covenant of union?

............, I take you to be my partner. All that I am I give to you, all that I have I share with you.

To make the marriage relationship clearer and more explicit, the vow can be modified to "partner in marriage" as in the Uniting Church of Australia's recently authorised *Additional Marriage Service* (2018). In this ceremony, the celebrant asks each partner:

............, will you give yourself to .... to be her/his/............'s marriage partner/husband/wife to live together in the covenant of marriage?

This Uniting Church of Australia ceremony is both admirable and distinctive as it is not identified or classified specifically as a same-sex marriage resource. The wording can be used by heterosexual couples who wish to avoid the patriarchal language, implied gender roles (e.g. wife/husband) and assumptions, which are present in more traditional ceremony formats.

This same *Additional Marriage Service* from the Uniting Church of Australia (2018) includes the option of receiving Holy Communion. That is to say, the marriage may take place in the context of The Sacrament of the Lord's Supper.

3 — The blessing of same-sex marriage

After many years of widespread consultation and discussion, the Anglican Church in Aotearoa, New Zealand and Polynesia now provides for the blessing by an Anglican priest (authorised by his or her bishop) for a same-sex couple who have previously entered a civil marriage. Some of this material is available below. These words and prayers can also be used to bless heterosexual civil marriages at the end of an "ordinary" marriage ceremonies.

Preliminary prayers

Celebrant:

> Faithful God, holy and eternal, hear us as we pray for .... and ....

> May their union be life-giving and life-long, enriched by your presence and strengthened by your grace; may they bring comfort and confidence to each other in tenderness, faithfulness, respect, and trust.

> God of love / E te Atua aroha

Congregation responds:

> Grant our prayer / Whakarongo mai ki tā mātou īnoi

Celebrant:

> May the hospitality of their home bring refreshment and joy to strangers and friends alike.

> May their love for each other in good times and bad overflow to neighbours in need.

> May they celebrate with the joyful, befriend the lonely, and comfort those in sorrow.

> God of love / E te Atua aroha

Congregation responds:

Grant our prayer / Whakarongo mai ki tā mātou īnoi

The Blessing of the Couple

The couple kneels. The celebrant prays one of the following:

Option 1

Celebrant:

Blessed are you, O God, ruler of the universe,
for you have created all things
and you surround us with signs of your faithfulness.
Pour now the abundance of your blessing on .... and
.... who have committed their lives to each other.
Let their love for each other be a seal upon their hearts
and a crown upon their heads.
Bless them in their work and in their companionship;
awake and asleep, in joy and in sorrow, in life and in death.

Finally, in your mercy,
bring them to that heavenly marriage feast,
where your saints feast for ever more.
Through Jesus Christ your Son, our Lord,
who lives and reigns with you and the Holy Spirit,
one God, now and for ever. Amen.

God the Father,
God the Son,
God the Holy Spirit,
bless, preserve, and keep you;
God grant you abundant grace
that, living together in faith and love,
you may be a blessing to each other
and may receive the blessings of eternal life. Amen.

Option 2

Most gracious God,
we praise you for the gift of human love.

We give you thanks for .... and ....,
and the promises of faithfulness they have made.
Pour out the abundance of your Holy Spirit upon them.
Keep them in your steadfast love;
protect them in all danger;
fill them with your wisdom and peace;
and lead them in service to each other and the world.

May the blessing of God the Father
God the Son, and God the Holy Spirit,
be with you and remain with you,
that you may always be a blessing to each other
and to all whom you meet. Amen.

Option 3

Eternal God,
you create us out of love
that we should love you and one another.
Bless .... and ...., each made in your image,
whose commitment to each other
is a sign of your faithful love to us
in Christ our Lord. Amen.

By your Holy Spirit,
fill them both with wisdom and hope
that they may delight in your gift of love
and enrich one another in love and steadfast faithfulness;
through Jesus Christ our Lord. Amen.

Bring them to that table
where your saints celebrate forever in your heavenly home;
through Jesus Christ our Lord,
who with you and the Holy Spirit lives and reigns,
one God, forever and ever. Amen.

Option 4

May God who has made a covenant with us
keep you in love with each other

so that you will be a sign
and an example of God's never-failing love.

May God give you friends and family
to help you live in peace with all people.

May you always bear witness to the love of God
so that the afflicted and the needy will find welcome in your home.

And may the Almighty God bless you: Father, Son and Holy Spirit.
Amen.

Part Five – Alternative language and religion options

1 — A Māori language ceremony
Te ritenga karakia mō te Mārena

Te reo Māori (The Māori language) is an official language of Aotearoa-New Zealand. The everyday use of te reo Māori has been increasing significantly over the last 30 years. Te reo Māori is a national and (international) treasure (taonga), and its revival is a priority.

We are very grateful to Rev Dr Wayne Te Kaawa for making "Ngā Whakaritenga Mārena" – a marriage order of service in te reo Māori – available for our book. Dr Te Kaawa is a Presbyterian minister and former Moderator of Te Aka Puaho (the Presbyterian Māori synod). He was the first Māori Chaplain at the University of Otago (2018-19) and is currently the inaugural lecturer in Māori theology at the University.

The content of the service is a Christian wedding service that incorporates Tikanga Māori at the beginning when a pōwhiri or welcoming ceremony is held (Te Whakaeke). Once this is completed the wedding service begins with the ringing of the bell which is a signal for the people to prepare to worship God.

To encourage the use of te reo Māori, we have chosen not to provide a complete translation. However, translation of some key terms is provided. You may like to incorporate portions of what is given here into your own ceremony, or make use of the entire ceremony in te reo Māori.

Ngā Whakaritenga Mārena
– order of marriage service/ceremony

Instructions are in *Italics*

Te Whakaeke (the arrival process/ kawa of the Marae)
Kei te noho a (te tāne) me tana ope ki te mahau o te whare.

Ka eke a (te wahine) me tana ope ki runga i te marae.

Ka whakatauria e te haukāinga

Ka whakautua e te kaikōrero mō te ope whakaeke.

Ka mutu ngā kōrero, ka hoatu te rākau kōrero ki te Minita

Ka patua ai te pere. (the bell is rung)

Te Minita (Minister / Celebrant)
Nei te karanga a te Atua ki te whānau o tā tātou puhi māreikura. Mauria mai tā tātou tamāhine kia honoa ai ia ki te hono a te Atua, e kore nei e wewete e te tangata...

Ka haria mai a .... ki te mahau e tōna matua.

Ka tangohia tana korowai ka whakahokia ki tōna matua.

He Mihi Whakatau (Welcome to the guests)
E oku hoa aroha, e ngā whanaunga, ngā mana, ngā reo kei waenganui i a tātou i tēnei rā. Nau mai, haere mai ki tēnei honoa, tēnei mārena a .... rāua ko ....

Te Karakia (Prayers)
Nō reira kia timatahia tēnei karakia i runga i te ingoa a Te Matua, a Te Tama, a Te Wairua Tapu. Amine.

Kia inoi tātou:

E Te Atua Kaha rawa, E whakapaingia nei ake ake, e tuohu ana mātou ki tou aroaro i tēnei rā. E whakawhetai ana mātou ki a koe e te Atua mō tēnei rā tino ātaahua, kia whakatata mai koe ki a mātou e Te Hēpara Pai.

Manaakitia te kaupapa a tēnei rā, a tēnei karakia e te Atua, he tohu o tou aroha ki a mātou, he tohu o te aroha kei waenganui o ēnei tokorua. Ko Ihu Karakia hoki tō mātou Ariki.

Amine.

Anei ētahi kōrero o ngā Karaipiture e pā ana ki te mārena (Scripture readings)

Nō Te Kawenata Tawhito: (Genesis 2:18)

> Nā ka mea a Ihowa te Atua, e kore e pai kia noho te tangata ko ia anake; me hanga e ahau tētahi hoa pai mōna. A, kawea ana e ia te wahine ki te tāne.

Nō Te Rongopai: (Matthew 19:5)

> Ka mea a Ihu, mō konei ka mahue i te tāne tōna pāpā, tōna whaea, ka piri ki tana wahine, ā, hei kikokiko kotahi rāua tokorua.

Nō Ngā Whakatauāki: (Proverbs 18:22)

> Te tangata kua kite i te wahine māna, kua kite i te mea pai, kua whiwhi anō ki tā Ihowa whakapai.

Minister / Celebrant to the couple:

> Atu i tēnei wā, me aro kōrua ki a kōrua, kia noho kōrua hei hoa pūmau kōrua mō ake tonu atu. Kia kaha tā kōrua whakahōnore, whakatenatena, tautoko anō a tētahi i tētahi. I ngā wā o te taumahatanga, mā kōrua anō kōrua e hāpai kia tutuki rawa ai i tā kōrua mārena tētahi āhua kihai i taea e te kotahi. Manaakitia tō kōrua aroha, ā, tohea ko tā kōrua hono hei hono tātai e kore e oti noa. I te pātukitanga o te manawa, me aroha kōrua ki a kōrua – tētahi ki tētahi.

I Koroniti 13:4-7 (1 Corinthians 13:4-7)

> He manawanui te aroha, ā, he atawhai;
> E kore te aroha e hae; e kore te aroha e whakahīhī,
> e kore e whakapehapeha
> Kāhore ōna tikanga whānoke, e kore e whai ki āna ake.

E kore e riri wawe, e kore e whakairi kino;
E kore e hari ki te hē, engari ka hari tahi me te pono
E whakamanawanui ana ki ngā mea katoa,
E whakapono ana ki ngā mea katoa
E tūmanako ana ki ngā mea katoa
E whakaririka kau ana ki ngā mea katoa.

Atu i tēnei wā (Tane name, Wahine name) me aro kōrua ki ngā rā kei mua i a kōrua

Atu i tēnei wā (Tane name, Wahine name) me aro kōrua ki a kōrua, tētahi ki tētahi

Atu i tēnei wā (Tane name, Wahine name) he hononga tēnei kei tua o tō te tinana hono

Mō kōrua te hono pūmau o te aroha, o te manaaki – he hono nō te Atua

Ahakoa kei a kōrua ngā rawa o te ao, kei te Atua tonu tō kōrua oranga

Atu i tēnei wā (Tane name, Wahine name) me aro kōrua ki tā kōrua mārena.

Pātai:

(*Preliminary question to the couple*:

Do you know of any reason why you should not be joined together in God?)

.... kōrua ko ....,

E mōhio rānei tētahi i tētahi take kia kaua ai kōrua e honoa ki te hono a te Atua?

Ki te kore, e tika ana kia haere tonu tātou

(If not, then it's right for us to continue).

Ngā Pātai (main questions to the couple)

Ki te Tāne:

Ka hono atu koe ki a .... hei wahine pūmau mōhou
Kia arohaina atu, kia whakahōnoretia e koe
I te wā o te mate, o te ora rānei
I ngā wā o te pai, o te kino rānei
Atu i tēnei rā, ā tutuki noa

Tāne: Ae!

Ki te Wahine:

Ka hono atu koe ki a .... hei tāne pūmau mōhou
Kia arohaina atu, kia whakahōnoretia e koe
I te wā o te mate, o te ora rānei
I ngā wā o te pai, o te kino rānei
Atu i tēnei rā, ā tutuki noa

Wahine: Ae!

Nā reira, kia noho ngā manaakitanga o te Atua ki runga i a kōrua, i a kōrua e tuku nei i ēnei oati tapu tētahi ki tētahi.

Kia tau te rangimārie o Te Atua ki runga i a kōrua.

Kia inoi Tātou (prayer)

E Te Atua Atawhai
Kia tau ngā manaakitanga ki runga i a .... rāua ko ....
Arahina rāua.

Homai ki a rāua te kaha ki te mau, ki te pupuri i ngā oati
Kia piki tonu ai tō rāua aroha ki a Koe, ki a rāua anō hoki
Kia kaha tonu atu te tipu i roto i a Ihu Karaiti, tō tātou Ariki.
Amine.

Ngā Oati Tapu (Vows/oaths)

Te Tāne:

E tono atu nei au ki a koutou katoa,
kia mātakihia mai koutou, e hono atu nei ahau (Tane name) i a (wahine name) hei wahine pūmau mōku

Te Wahine: (reply)

>Ko tōku katoa ka tuku nei ki a koe
>ko aku rawa katoa ka hoatu ki a koe.
>Ahakoa te aha, ka aroha ahau ki a koe, kia tū tahi ai tāua,
>ā tutuki noa, ko taku oati tēnei ka hoatu ki a koe

Te Wahine:

>E tono atu nei au ki a koutou katoa
>kia mātakihia mai koutou, e hono atu nei ahau – (Wahine name) i a (Tāne name) hei tāne pūmau mōku

Te Tāne: (reply)

>Ko tōku katoa ka tuku nei ki a koe
>ko aku rawa katoa ka hoatu ki a koe.
>Ahakoa te aha, ka aroha ahau ki a koe, kia tū tahi ai tāua,
>ā tutuki noa, ko taku oati tēnei ka hoatu ki a koe

Ngā Rīngi (The giving and receiving of rings)

Ka waiho ngā ringi ki runga i te Paipera Tapu – the rings are placed on the Holy Bible

The blessing of the rings:

>Kia inoi tātou – kia whakapaingia ēnei rīngi hei tohu i te aroha o tētahi ki tētahi. He rite tonu ki tō te Atua aroha ki a tātou – kāore tōna timatanga, kāore tōna mutunga.
>
>E te Matua, Tama, Wairua Tapu, anei ngā taonga o te aroha. Whakatapua ēnei taonga o te aroha mō te painga o Ihu Karaiti, tō mātou Ariki. Amine.

Te Tāne:

>(Wahine name) ka hoatu nei au i tēnei rīngi ki a koe
>hei tohu i tō tāua aroha me ngā oati tapu kua whakapuakina ake i te rā nei

Te Wahine:

>Ae, e tango nei au i tēnei rīngi, hei tohu i tō tāua aroha me ngā oati tapu kua whakapuakina ake i te rā nei

Te Wahine:

> (Tāne name) ka hoatu nei au i tēnei rīngi ki a koe hei tohu i tō tāua aroha me ngā oati tapu kua whakapuakina ake i te rā nei

Te Tāne:

> Ae, e tango nei au i tēnei rīngi,
> hei tohu i tō tāua aroha me ngā oati tapu kua whakapuakina ake i te rā nei

Te Whakapai (Prayer of Blessing)

> E Te Matua o tō mātou Ariki a Ihu Karaiti.
> Kia tau tō manaaki,
> kia ū tonu hoki ki runga i tēnei tāne me tēnei wahine.
> Manaakitia tō rāua mārena.
> Arahina, whangaia, tautokona rāua i roto o tō rāua oranga.
> Tukua mai ki a rāua te ora me te rangimārie i ngā wā katoa e ora ai rāua.
> Ā, i a rāua e puta atu nei ki te ao, hei tāne pūmau, hei wahine pūmau
>
> Mā te Atua kōrua e manaaki, e tiaki
> Māna anō te māramatanga o tōna kanohi e whakawhiti nei ki runga i a kōrua
> Mā te Atua kōrua e arataki ki ōna ara
>
> Kia tau ai tōna rangimārie ki runga i a kōrua i ngā rā katoa e ora ai kōrua. Amine.

He Waiata (song or hymn)

Te Inoi a Te Ariki (The Lord's Prayer)

> E tō mātou Matua i te rangi
> Kia tapu tou ingoa
> Kia tae mai tou rangatiratanga
> Kia meatia tāu e pai ai ki runga ki te whenua kia rite anō ki tō te rangi.
> Homai kia mātou, aianei, he taro mō mātou mo tēnei ra.

Murua ō mātou hara
me mātou hoki e muru nei i o te hunga e hara ana ki a mātou
Aua hoki mātou e kawea kia whakawaia
Engari whakaorangia mātou i te kino
Nou hoki te Rangatiratanga
Te kaha me te korōria
Ake ake ake
Amine.

Te Waitohu i te Raihana Mārena (signing the marriage register)

Ka hainatia ai te raihana e te rāngai mārena (Te wahine me te tāne, Te Mīnita, me ngā kaitaunaki) – signing by groom, bride, minister and witnesses.

Te Whakatau (Declaration of Marriage)

.... kōrua ko .... kua whakaaturia tō kōrua aroha
I mua i te aroaro o ō kōrua whānau me ō kōrua hoa
Kua whakapuakina mai he oati tapu
Ā, kua whakatinanahia ai tēnei mā te hono i ngā ringa
me te tuku i ngā rīngi
Mā te mana kua ūhia nei au e te Hāhi me te Karauna
(with the authority bestowed upon me by the Church and the Crown/State)
Māku anō kōrua e whakatau: (I declare to you both)
Hei Tāne, Hei Wahine Pūmau: (You are man and woman together, permanently, forever)

2 — A Buddhist (Tibetan) marriage ceremony

Within every great world religion, including Buddhism, there are many different groupings and traditions, with all sorts of variations in culture and form. Greg Hughson was privileged to officiate at this Buddhist wedding ceremony which was held outdoors in the Dunedin Botanic Gardens. The words come largely from Lama Yeshe (now deceased). Their ceremony structure, provided here, is an example of how the faith held by a couple can be incorporated into their wedding. In this case, the ceremony began with five minutes of Buddhist Tara prayer, chanted by a group of Geshes (Tibetan Buddhist Monks). The bride and groom chose not only to commit their lives to each other, but also to express their commitment to living out their lives in accordance with the basic teachings of the Buddhist faith. These teachings, very appropriately, were included in this unique and very special order of service.

Wedding Format

The wedding venue may be either outdoors, or indoors.

The bride walks in (with her father), to suitable music

Chants

Heart Sutra recitation, short Tara prayer, abbreviated Buddha meditation

Welcome and introduction

Celebrant:

Buddhism is a path of transformation of one's inner potential and it is a path dedicated to serving others, helping them awaken their potential.

Marriage provides the context within which to practice serving others.

Love is desiring a lifetime of happiness for each other.

Marriage is an equal commitment to the happiness of each partner, and a commitment towards enabling each other's' awakening.

Our inner potential is developed through taking on challenges, not just through joy.

We need each other in marriage, and in all relationships, in order to practice compassion.

Since a Buddhist marriage is dedicated toward the happiness of all living beings, those gathered here are representatives of all living beings.

Reading as chosen by the couple

The Questions

Celebrant:

.... and .... are happy today not only because they can share the joy of their love for each other with friends and family, but also because they have the opportunity to express their aspirations for the future.

.... and ...., do you pledge to help each other to develop your hearts and minds, cultivating compassion, generosity, ethics, patience, enthusiasm, concentration and wisdom as you age and undergo the various ups and downs of life and to transform them into the path of love, compassion, joy and equanimity?

Groom and Bride: We do

Celebrant:

Recognizing that the external conditions in life will not always be smooth and that internally your own minds and emotions will sometimes get stuck in negativity. Do you pledge to see all these circumstances as a challenge to help you grow, to open your hearts, to accept yourselves, and each other; and to generate compassion for others who are suffering? Do you pledge to avoid becoming narrow, closed or opinionated, and to help each other to see various sides of situations?

Groom and Bride: We do

Celebrant:

Understanding that just as we are a mystery to ourselves, each other person is also a mystery to us. Do you pledge to seek to understand yourselves, each other, and all living beings, to examine your own minds continually and to regard all the mysteries of life with curiosity and joy?

Groom and Bride: We do

Celebrant:

Do you pledge to preserve and enrich your affection for each other, and to share it with all beings? To take the loving feelings you have for one another and your vision of each other's potential and inner beauty as an example and rather than spiralling inwards and becoming self-absorbed, to radiate this love outwards to all beings?

Groom and Bride: We do

Celebrant:

Do you pledge to remember the kindness of all other beings and your connection to them? Do you pledge to work for the welfare of others, with all of your compassion, wisdom and skill?

Groom and Bride: We do

Celebrant:

Do you pledge day-to-day, to be patient with yourselves and others, knowing that change comes slowly and gradually, and to seek inspiration from your teachers not to become discouraged?

Groom and Bride: We do

Celebrant:

> Do you pledge to continuously strive to remember your own Buddha nature, as well as the Buddha nature of all living beings? To maintain the awareness that all things are temporary, and to remain optimistic that you can achieve your greatest potential and lasting happiness?

Groom and Bride: We do

The Vows (*as provided or chosen by the couple*)

The exchange of rings

Celebrant:

> Having committed to these vows, do you, ..., take ...., to be your legal wife?

Groom: I do

Celebrant:

> Having committed to these vows, do you, ..., take .... to be your legal husband?

Bride: I do.

Celebrant:

> .... and ...., these wedding rings are symbols of your love, and will forever remind you of the vows that you have made today.

Groom:

> .... I give you this ring in token of the vows we have made together, and as a sign of my love and affection for you.

Bride:

> .... I give you this ring in token of the vows we have made together, and as a sign of my love and affection for you.

Pronouncement of Marriage

Celebrant:

Suitable words of pronouncement, followed by, to the Groom: "and you may kiss the bride."

Concluding Dedication (*may be recited by all present*)

Note: Dedication of merits/positive energy is important at the end of Buddhist practice.

May all beings everywhere,
Plagued by sufferings of body and mind,
Obtain an ocean of happiness and joy
By virtue of my merits.

May no living creature suffer,
Commit evil or ever fall ill.
May no one be afraid or belittled,
With a mind weighed down by depression.

May the blind see forms
And the deaf hear sounds.
May those whose bodies are worn with toil
Be restored on finding repose.

May the naked find clothing,
The hungry find food.
May the thirsty find water
And delicious drinks.

May the poor find wealth,
Those weak with sorrow find joy.
May the forlorn find hope,
Constant happiness and prosperity.

May there be timely rains
And bountiful harvests.
May all medicines be effective
And wholesome prayers bear fruit.

May all who are sick and ill
Quickly be freed from their ailments.
Whatever diseases there are in the world,
May they never occur again.

May the frightened cease to be afraid
And those bound be freed.
May the powerless find power
And may people think of benefiting each other.

For as long as space remains,
For as long as sentient beings remain,
Until then, may I too remain,
To dispel the misery of the world.

Signing of the register

Wedding party photos, followed by reception.

3 — Muslim marriage

Islam stretches across a diverse range of politics and cultures with followers and practices as varied as the countries from which they come. Marriage in Islam is viewed as a religious obligation and a solemn contract between the husband and wife. It is considered an act of worship. Whether you are planning a Muslim wedding or attending your first Muslim wedding, it is important to understand both historic and cultural Muslim wedding traditions.

The only requirement for Muslim weddings is the signing of a Muslim marriage contract. This is signed by both the groom and bride who decide on the detailed content of the contract. What is consistent in all contracts however, is acknowledgement of the centrality of Allah (God) and obedience to Allah. This is included in the contract between the bride and the groom. Muslim marriage traditions vary, depending on culture. In some Muslim countries where Islam permits a man to marry more than one wife, the bride may include a clause in the marriage contract specifying that her husband must not have any other wives.

When a marriage is held in a mosque, men and women may choose to remain separate during the ceremony and reception. The Imam of the mosque or indeed any Muslim who understands Islamic tradition, can officiate a wedding. The New Zealand Marriage licence can be signed during a Muslim wedding ceremony, or a few days or weeks afterwards; in effect, as with many European countries, the religious dimension is separate to the civil legal dimension of establishing a marriage.

A *mahr* (dowry) is part of every Muslim marriage contract. It may be in two parts. First, the *muqaddam*, or the prompt *mahr*, which the wife must receive at or immediately after the marriage ceremony. The second, called the *mu'akhar*, is a deferred and promised amount, payable at any agreed upon date following the consummation of the marriage. Often the deferred amount is larger than the amount paid at marriage. Traditionally, the deferred amount is supposed to provide the wife with a means of support, and is associated with the death or divorce of the husband. However, this is a more traditional rather than a religious stance on the matter. The *mu'akhar* should be viewed as important as the initial dowry payment as it is an obligation to be fulfilled by the husband. It is considered a debt if it is not given to the wife within the time-frame agreed upon between the couple. Receiving the *mahr* as specified in any Islamic marriage contract is a fundamental religious right of the wife. Upon the husband's death, any deferred *mahr* is to be paid from his estate to his wife before all other debts. This is regarded as a religious requirement.

The Nikah (Muslim marriage contract ceremony)

The marriage contract is signed at a nikah ceremony in which the groom, or his representative, proposes to the bride in front of at least two witnesses, stating the details of the *mahr*.

The bride and groom demonstrate their free will by repeating the word *qabul* (Arabic for "I accept") three times. Then the couple and two male witnesses sign the contract, making the marriage legal according to religious law. After its registration with the government authorities, it becomes official.

During the Nikah ceremony, in some Islamic traditions, a male representative (usually bride's father or uncle), called a *wali*, acts on the bride's behalf. In some other traditions, the bride should represent herself. Sometimes, if the bride is not present in the place where nikah ceremony is being conducted, two witnesses (usually family members or relatives of the bride) will go to her and ask her consent to the marriage. Then they return to the ceremony and testify to that effect to the person who is officiating, in front of the two marriage witnesses.

Sample of a simple Muslim marriage contract:

We, the undersigned, (Groom) and (Bride) have agreed on this ...... day in the month of .... the year of .... to the following terms so that Almighty Allah may bless our marriage and make it endure with happiness.

We marry in the name of Allah, the Creator of the Universe.

We agree that the Groom will give the Bride the following Mahr (*details inserted*)

Our marriage shall be in accordance to Shari'ah, our children shall be raised as Muslims, and our living habits (inside and outside the home) shall be in accordance with Islam.

We understand marriage is a strong covenant before Allah. We shall strive always to maintain this covenant through constant devotion to Him and dedication to our relationship.

We the undersigned pray to Allah to help us honour this contract, and we take Allah, the Lord of the Universe, as our Witness. We make this pledge and agreement in front of the following witnesses:

Signatures

> Groom:
>
> Bride:
>
> Wali:
>
> Witness:
>
> Witness:
>
> Imam (Officiant /Celebrant):
>
> Date:

Vows and Blessings

The Imam will usually offer an additional religious ceremony following the nikah, which includes a recitation of the Fatihah – the first chapter of the Quran – and Du'a (blessings). Most Muslim couples do not recite vows. Rather, they listen as the Imam speaks about the meaning of marriage and their responsibilities to each other and Allah. However, some Muslim brides and grooms do say vows, such as this common example:

Groom:

> I, ... propose to marry you in accordance with the instructions of the Holy Quran and the Prophet Mohamed, peace and blessing be upon him. I pledge, in honesty and with sincerity, to be for you an obedient and faithful husband.

Bride:

> I sincerely accept and pledge, in honesty and sincerity, to be for you a faithful and helpful wife.

What Guests Should Wear to a Muslim Wedding

Different Muslim families have different levels of comfort when it comes to what they consider appropriate clothing for a wedding. If you are attending a Muslim wedding ceremony and are not sure how to dress, err on the side of modesty. Men and women should cover their legs and arms. Women may be asked to wear a head covering, especially in a mosque. Women should choose dresses or tops with a modest neckline. If you still are not sure what to wear, ask the bride or groom.

The Bride's Wedding Outfit

In many cultures, the Muslim bride changes into a special gown after the wedding ceremony is complete. This is a beautiful sight to behold, especially for guests attending their first Muslim wedding.

Separating Genders

Gender separation is a normal part of many Muslim traditions, including Muslim wedding traditions. Not every Muslim couple will choose to separate the genders at their wedding, but more traditional ceremonies will keep men and women apart.

During the reception, men and women may celebrate in different rooms, be divided by a partition or simply sit at different tables. In some cases, non-Muslim guests may be seated with opposite genders. If you are at a Muslim wedding where the genders are separated, respect the custom and don't initiate interactions with someone from the opposite sex.

The Wedding Feast (Walima)

Get ready for food. Lots of it. After the wedding contract is signed, it's time to feast. This is called the *Walima*, and it may feature traditional symbols of fertility and plenty, like fish, chicken, rice and candy-covered almonds. In some Muslim cultures, the *walima* lasts for more than one day, so make sure your clothes have some stretch to them! Guests should also be aware that the Muslim faith forbids the consumption of alcohol. Do not expect any champagne toasts at a traditional Muslim wedding.

Appendices

1 — Hymn, song and musical options

The singing of a hymn or song, sometimes two, very occasionally three or more, is a common feature of many weddings. It is not essential to have any public singing, but singing can and often does help unite everyone present and build a sense of community. Appropriate songs, hymns, and/or a musical item during the ceremony, contribute variety and a refreshing break from spoken words only. Recorded music, or quiet organ music, can also be played before the ceremony to help create a relaxed atmosphere.

One option to aid singing is to arrange for a well known recorded song to be played, and to invite everyone to sing along. Sometimes, a band (guitars, drums etc) can be arranged to accompany the singing – a way of involving friends and/or a Church worship team.

Your ceremony could also be enhanced by including a musical item. One or more of your talented friends could contribute to your ceremony, perhaps with a song, or an instrumental item. Sometimes, a choir can be arranged to sing something appropriately inspiring and uplifting.

Another popular option is to have a special musical item performed by a friend or friends during the signing of the register. Alternatively, carefully chosen recorded music can be played during the signing of the register, and to conclude the ceremony as the wedding party process out.

There are a large number of potentially suitable songs, hymns and musical items. If you are familiar with a particular hymn book, or already have a favourite hymn and/or contemporary worship song in mind, then you can include these. If you are not sure just what kind of song or hymn is suitable, have a look through the small selection we provide here. These can be found in the *With One Voice* (WOV) hymn book, in *Alleluia Aotearoa* (AA) or in *Together in Song*:

Australian Hymn Book II (TIS). Many of these hymns and songs will also be found in other hymn and song books.

First, a few hymns of the more traditional nature:

- *The Lord's my Shepherd* (WOV 16), to the tune Crimond, is a well-known hymn and therefore frequently chosen. However, it is also often used at funerals, which may mean that it brings to mind sad occasions for some who sing it during a wedding.
- *O Perfect Love* (WOV 526), and *O God, from whom...'* (WOV 566), are two traditional wedding hymns, fairly well known in church circles, but likely to seem rather dated in style and language.

Alternatively, there are a number of tried and tested general hymns that can be used.

In this category we would suggest:

- *Father, Hear the Prayer we Offer* (WOV 510)
- *Praise my Soul, the King of Heaven* (WOV 68)
- *For the Beauty of the Earth* (WOV 77)
- *Love divine, all loves excelling* (WOV 148)

If you feel you would like to try a hymn that is more contemporary, then we would suggest:

- *Come to a wedding* (AA 25)
- *Come on this wedding day* (AA 24)
- *God gave to man the woman, and to the woman gave the man* (AA 46)
- *Sing Praise and Thanksgiving* (WOV 25)
- *The Great Love of God* (WOV 105)
- *He Came Singing Love* (WOV 636)

Other suitable hymn options from *Together in Song: Australian Hymn Book II* (TIS), many of which will be in other hymn books such as *With One Voice* (WOV) include:

- *All creatures of our God and King* (TIS 100)
- *Brother, sister, let me serve you* (TIS 650)
- *Come down, O Love divine* (TIS 398)
- *Come, Holy Spirit, Lord of grace* (TIS 403)
- *In faith and hope and love* (TIS 628)
- *Joyful, joyful we adore you* (TIS 152)
- *Lord of all hopefulness* (TIS 613)
- *May the mind of Christ my Saviour* (TIS 609)
- *Now thank we all our God* (TIS 106)
- *Your love, O God, has called us here* (TIS 664)

All of the above hymns are suitable as religious/spiritual wedding songs. Although not widely known, they are generally easy enough to sing, and worth the effort if you like the words.

Morning has Broken (WOV 91) is another possibility. This is widely used because the tune is quite well-known. Alternatively, you can sing the following words to the tune of *Morning has Broken* (Bunessan):

A Wedding Song

> Standing together, facing the future
> Sure of each other, glad in our love
> Say hope is golden, say it is dream time;
> Pray for our future, pray for our love.

> Standing together, promising truly:
> We will be steadfast, we understand.
> Say love is sunshine, say its enchanting;
> Pray for our future, pray for our love.

> Life is for sharing, life is for giving
> Now and for ever, near or away
> Standing together, each will be strengthened;
> Pray for our marriage, pray for our love.

Beyond these suggestions there are many other options and online resources from which you can select a song or hymn. You can print the words for the songs/hymns in your wedding sheet, or project them onto a screen during your ceremony.

2 — Website / Internet resources

The following is a list of websites and internet resources that have been consulted in preparing this book, to which we may have referred, or else recommend as an option to seek further resources. It is by no means exhaustive. A general internet search will reveal much more.

New Zealand celebrants

- https://celebrants.dia.govt.nz/
- https://www.celebrantsassociation.co.nz/

Practical information

Births, Deaths and Marriages = Whānautanga, Matenga, Mārenatanga

- https://www.govt.nz/organisations/births-deaths-and-marriages/
- https://www.govt.nz/browse/family-and-whanau/getting-married/get-a-marriage-licence/
- https://marriages.services.govt.nz/
- https://prepare-enrich.co.nz/articles/articles-for-couples
- https://www.govt.nz/browse/family-and-whanau/separating-or-getting-divorced/relationship-counselling/

Ceremony information

See the document *Thanksgiving for the birth of a Child* on the Methodist Church of Aotearoa–New Zealand's website:

- http://www.methodist.org.nz/faith_and_order

Uniting Church of Australia Marriage services:

- https://assembly.uca.org.au/marriage-services

Same-sex resources

Anglican report (2014) The Way Forward

- http://www.anglican.org.nz/content/download/41423/209336/file/WayForwardReportFINAL201420Feb.docx

Hansard NZ Government Marriage (Definition of Marriage) amendment bill – first reading

- https://www.parliament.nz/en/pb/hansard-debates/rhr/document/50HansD_20120829_00000032/marriage-definition-of-marriage-amendment-bill-first

Muslim marriage contract

Muslim contract (pp 162-163) was sourced from:

- https://www.ictucson.org/

Children's ceremony

Rochelle Fleming:

- https://www.nzweddingcelebrant.co.nz/contact
- https://www.nzweddingcelebrant.co.nz/single-post/2016/06/15/Welcome-baby-%E2%80%93-naming-ceremonies

3 — References

This list contains information on books and other resources we have referred to in our text.

Agnew, P. (2004). *Heartsongs – readings for weddings.* Random House New Zealand

Alleluia Aotearoa, The NZ Hymnbook Trust.

Anglican Church of Aotearoa-New Zealand, (2016). "A Way Forward – He Anga Whakamua – Na Sala ki Liu" Recommendations to General Synod / te Hīnota Whānui 2016. (See website list).

Book of Common Order, Church of Scotland.

Book of Common Worship, Presbyterian Church, USA.

Book of Worship, 2nd Edition. United Church of Christ (USA).

Bracken Long, K., and D. Maxwell (2015). *Inclusive marriage services – a wedding sourcebook.* Westminster John Knox Press. (Print and Kindle versions available).

Bracken Long, K. (2016). *From this day forward. Rethinking the Christian wedding.* Westminster John Knox Press. (Print and Kindle versions available).

Celebrate God's Presence, United Church of Canada.

Ellison, M. M. (2004) *Same Sex Marriage? A Christian Ethical Analysis*, Pilgrim Press.

Foley, M. P. (2008). *Wedding Rites.* Eerdmans Publishing Co. (Appendix includes list of Wedding Album recordings and CD's)

Gushee, D. P. with B.D. McLaren, P. Tickle and M. Vines (2014). *Changing our mind.* Read the Spirit Books.

Salz, Victor (1974). *Between Husband and Wife.* Paulist Press.

The Alternative Marriage Book, Northstone Publishing (1995)

Together in Song: Australian Hymn Book, HarperCollinsReligious.

With One Voice, with NZ Supplement, Collins.

4 — Bibliography of same-sex resources

We provide this bibliography primarily for theological students, clergy, religious leaders and others interested in exploring further the theological basis for the blessing of same-sex marriages.

Adam, A K A. "Disciples Together, constantly." In Seow, *Homosexuality and Christian Community*. (Louisville: Westminster John Knox Press, 1996)

Barth, Karl. *The Humanity of God* (Louisville: Westminster John Knox Press, 1996)

Brownson, James V. *Bible, gender, sexuality: reframing the Church's debate on same-sex relationships* (Michigan: Eerdmans, 2013). (Print and Kindle versions available).

Coakley, Sarah. *God, sexuality and the self: and essay 'on the Trinity'* (Cambridge: Cambridge University Press, 2019)

Farley, Margaret A. *Just love: a framework for Christian Sexual Ethics* (New York: Continuum, 2012).

Hatchett, Marion J. *Commentary on the American Prayer Book* (New York: Harper Collins, 1995).

Hefling Charles (ed). *Our Selves, Our Souls and Bodies: sexuality and the household of God* (Cambridge, Mass: Cowley, 1996).

Jordan, Mark D (ed). *Authorizing marriage? Canon, tradition, and critique in the blessing of same sex unions.* (Princeton: Princeton University Press, 2006).

Jordan, Mark D. *Blessing same sex unions: the perils of queer romance and the confusions of Christian marriage.* (Chicago: University of Chicago Press, 2013).

Loughlin, Gerard. "Introduction: The End of Sex." In Gerard Loughlin (ed), *Queer Theology: Rethinking the Western Body*. (Oxford: Blackwell Publishing, 2007).

Rogers, Eugene F. *Sexuality and the Christian body: their way into the triune God* (Oxford: Blackwell Publishing, 1999).

Rogers, Eugene F. (ed). *Theology and Sexuality: classic and contemporary readings*. (Oxford: Blackwell, 2002).

Saliers, Don E. *Worship as Theology: foretaste of glory divine*. (Nashville: Abingdon, 1994).

Searle, Mark and Kenneth W. Stevenson. *Documents of the marriage liturgy*. (Collegeville: The Liturgical Press, 1992).

Seow, Choon-Leong (ed). *Homosexuality and Christian Community* (Louisville: Westminster John Knox Press, 1996).

Stevenson, Kenneth. *The nuptial blessing: a study of Christian marriage rites*. (London: SPCK, 1982).

Trible, P. *God and the Rhetoric of Sexuality*. (Philadelphia: Fortress, 1978).

Williams, Rowan. "The Body's Grace." In Hefling, *Our Selves, Our Souls and Bodies* pp 58-68. (Cambridge, Mass: Cowley, 1996).

www.ingramcontent.com/pod-product-compliance
Lightning Source LLC
Chambersburg PA
CBHW072020070526
44583CB00015B/1561